Man Up!

The Fatherly Advice

That Made Me The Woman That I Am Today

Lauren Washington

Contents

Dedication

I dedicate this book to my incarcerated father, who taught me the strength of resilience even in the face of adversity. Your love and unwavering support continue to inspire me every day.

In loving memory of my grandmother, Harmony (1951-2023). Your wisdom, kindness, and enduring love will live forever in my heart. You were the guiding light in my life, and I cherish the beautiful memories we shared.

Acknowledgment

I express my profound gratitude and appreciation to God, who has made all things possible in my life. I acknowledge that my Lord has carried me through all my days and never left me.

I extend a heartfelt thanks to my collaborator, J.C. Williams, whose strict approach has brought out the best in me for this project. Your validation of the lessons I learned from my father is commendable, and we need more men like you in this world.

I also want to thank my wonderful family and friends for their unwavering support, particularly my mother and Madison, for their valuable feedback on the manuscript and their continuous encouragement during tough times. My brother, known as "Bruh," is a pillar of strength and has been my biggest fan. You are such a great reminder of our dad, and I love you dearly. My cousin Kiesh, thank you for being a constant source of grounding and stability in my life.

Lastly, I want to pay tribute to my dad, LeRoy "Saalih" Washington, who has been my sole inspiration for writing this book. "You are me, and I am you!" Your love and teachings have been instrumental in shaping who I am today, and I cannot thank you enough. Even though you are not physically with us, you are always a part of our lives. I love you with all my heart.

~ The future holds great things!

Lauren "Pooh" Washington

About the Author

Lauren, a powerhouse with degrees in Real Estate and Business Administration, is currently on her MBA journey. Beyond academia, she co-founded the life-changing Anti-Bully Crusader's Organization in Texas. Not just an academic star, Lauren's co-authored the ABC Workbook and Facilitators Manual, and her upcoming book, "Man Up! The Fatherly Advice that Made Me the Woman I Am Today," is a game-changer.

Success has been her companion, but she's also known the taste of setbacks, fueling her drive as a focused entrepreneur. She lives by the mantra, "Every generation must prep for the next, tomorrow's the vision." Her father's influence, despite his incarceration since her childhood, instilled in her a profound duty to use her potential for good. She passionately believes that we're blessed beyond measure and must do more for those without a voice.

In her upcoming book, Lauren candidly shares her life's invaluable lessons from her father—love, failures, betrayals, and triumphant moments. Her aim? To inspire positive change by sharing her experiences and insights, adding "Author" to her list of remarkable achievements. Lauren's journey is a testament to determination, empathy, and her unyielding commitment to making a difference.

Chapter One:
No Political Party Affiliation

I N THE YEAR 2022, I found myself back in the classroom, working on my MBA. It was the first in-person semester since the pandemic hit, and as I sat in my political science class, I couldn't help but notice how different things were. The familiar faces of my fellow students were now covered with masks, and the air was thick with uncertainty and trepidation.

As the last week before finals approached, I began to realize that I was a little older than my classmates. Many of them already had the distinctive look and attitudes of future politicians—the kind of privilege that I had never experienced. I wondered who they would align themselves with and whether they would be the progressive thinkers that America so desperately needs.

I had absolutely no desire to enter the field of politics myself. But as I looked around the classroom, I realized that we were all there for the same reasons. Our individual plights may have been different, but no one's diploma indicated their personal struggles.

And really, does anyone else care what you go through to reach your goals?

In that moment, I thought to myself, *Damn, why did I take this class? I really have a strong dislike for American politics!* But little did I know, things were about to get exciting.

***

EVEN DISCUSSING POLITICS IS an exercise that inflames my passions and tests my temperament like nothing else.

I don't know if it's always been like this before my generation, but I find it utterly distasteful that the very people responsible for the continued advancement of our social liberties (cultural, educational, and financial freedoms) can only think of their political party's agendas. What adult entrusted with the responsibility of representing "the People" could logically endorse this approach to providing solutions for humanity?

Both Republicans and Democrats are guilty of this nonsense. What happened to putting the needs of "We the People" first? Instead of a collective brain trust, party affiliation has become membership to a legitimized gang! Democracy only works when "the People" dictate the agenda of the government. Tyranny exists when the government dictates the agenda of the people. Remember that!

It saddens me when I hear American people beefing like the Hatfields and McCoys over politics. The kicker being that the positions taken are often dictated to them. The "People" have had their consent manufactured to the point that even the idea of "taxation without representation" (the reason for America becoming independent of Britain) is deemed "normal."

Surely, we need taxes to support the system of public works that we all enjoy. However, how does the "government" (a group of ordinary people hiding behind concepts that predate New-Age logic) propose that even dead people pay taxes? Have you taken the time to consider the absurdity of the "Death Tax" or the "Estate Tax" or whichever ridiculous name they use to say that once a person dies, the living beneficiary must relinquish a portion of the estate for tax purposes?

Didn't those dead people pay taxes while they were alive? State taxes, Federal taxes, county taxes, income taxes, property taxes, sales tax, and whatever new tax they invent on the fly? Which party is responsible for endorsing that ingenious agenda? Instead of progressive leadership, the agenda has become: "Whoever loses gets the shorter end of the stick." Thus, whether right or wrong, you blindly stand behind your party's agenda simply because that's the cost of membership. Sounds like a gang, crew, outfit, squad, clique, or syndicate to me! (Not even a smart one.)

Here is a prime example of dumb American politics...

In 2022, in a 6-3 decision, the United States Supreme Court voted to overturn the decades-old Roe v. Wade ruling that created the Constitutional right to abortion in the US. This issue had already been decided by a previous Supreme Court, who apparently viewed the decision associated with this medical procedure to be a legitimate right of women to choose. However, the man behind the curtain can change his mind on a whim.

In response to the new ruling, the Court's only three liberal Justices filed dissenting opinions. We all know that dissenting opinions have no effect on the law and are typically written by the losing party. Roe v. Wade, decided in 1973, was a landmark case that granted women in all fifty states the right to control their own reproductive health choices.

As the result of the reversed ruling, the right to abortion will now be left up to each individual state's discretion. This represents the backward thinking of a supposedly forward-moving society. The highest Court in the land has essentially taken an equally protective blanket of legal authority and traded it for the possibility of overreaching regulations and confusion among American citizens.

Although we knew this was coming after the leak of Justice Alito's draft decision, that didn't make it any less shocking or unnerving. How do we process the idea that American women will lose a fundamental right that they've had for nearly five decades?

For millions of Americans this isn't just some abstract commentary about social issues. These aren't merely kitchen table concerns. This is about the freedom of choice, personal health, and the ability to live without intrusive government dictatorship.

We all have our own personal beliefs about abortion. In my opinion, the decision to abort a pregnancy is a deeply personal one that should not be controlled by the government. If ever there was an example of treading the "slippery slope" of legal authority, this is it.

Perhaps the next Constitutional Amendment to be repealed or reconsidered will be the right of citizens to own private property. Communism as a concept. Eminent Domain on a whole new level... what about that?

Just to drop a few jewels on those of you who are so gung-ho to associate yourselves with either political party, bar none. You are a slave to a system that has ZERO regard for your American citizenship, Bill of Rights, or value as a human, owning the freedom of choice. In fact, even if you "own" your home, you can never escape making payments. Aren't your property taxes perpetual? Hmmm? If you own the land, why do you owe anybody taxes? Wouldn't that be synonymous with paying taxes on furniture that you've purchased outright?

Moreover, even the outright ownership of a vehicle demands that you pay annual taxes for the renewal of license plates. Just for kicks, you must also purchase and pay insurance in perpetuity. Why? What is the government's interest in demanding that you purchase and maintain insurance from a private company? What authority supports the logic behind private citizens being subject to criminal prosecution for failure to do so? If this meets the definition of "ownership," then it's no wonder we mistake dictatorship for democracy.

Just food for thought for those of you who would disregard my opinion on the subject before considering its validity.

***

THERE IS A BIG difference between adhering to your own personal beliefs and forcing others to abide by them. Personally, I don't believe in or support abortion. However, I do believe in the right of choice. Our First Amendment Constitutional right says, "An individual has the right to worship God to his own dictates." This means, As long as your choice of worship doesn't violate the law (e.g., human sacrifice, confiscating land, etc.) or infringe upon another's right to worship, then you can worship anything you choose! It's your choice!

In addition, you may change your religious preference—without consequence, interference by laws, government, or politics—as often as you choose. God could have made us all Jewish, Christian, or Muslim, but he didn't! He gave us the free will to select whichever ideology and doctrine we choose to follow. Clearly, free choice is a very important aspect of human life. Thus, I view the issue of abortion similarly to God's constitution: freedom to choose one's own beliefs.

I seriously wonder whether this abuse of power, by an unelected group of conservative judges, will be the beginning of a trend in which party majorities feel entitled to overturn laws implemented by the opposing party strictly for political reasons or personal belief systems. As sad as this may sound, this is the precedent that is being set today in American politics.

I believe that the law, written in Latin, is meant to keep the ignorant majority unable to decipher or challenge the contracts that bind them to the system. In fact, the word "precedent" is foremost in legal terms, superseding "plain language" as the principle by which law is interpreted. In other words, "precedent" is supported by the way things have been done routinely—not exactly as they were written (which is why different states have different laws, supposedly interpreted from the one Constitution).

For the record, I will reiterate... it is my belief that no matter our personal views on abortion, HEALTH—not politics—should be the driving factor for medical decisions. As with the majority of Americans, I agree that abortion is a decision for a woman to make with a medical professional whom she trusts.

***

IN LIGHT OF MY views I wrote a paper expressing my opinion on this controversial topic. My Political Science professor put me on the spot right in front of my fellow classmates and asked me, "Well, Ms. Washington, what would you have us (society) do to fix this problem?"

"Which one?" I fired back, thinking he severely underestimated me if he thought I didn't have a comeback.

"Clearly, your issue is not about abortion," he said, in his usual condescending "I'm superior to you" tone.

I stood and answered. "Because our laws of civic participation are predicated upon age—eighteen or twenty-one—to enjoin in or enjoy the privilege of certain rights & liberties (but not punishments), I'd first start by making it illegal for anyone over the age of sixty-five to hold any office in America. Seniors would be restricted to teaching, consulting, and grooming the youthful and vibrant minds of our society to lead. I'd establish an Elder Council, like it was with older civilizations."

"Well, obviously that worked out well for them," he said in a joking, but sarcastic manner.

Some of my classmates found that amusing. I didn't find anything funny about his elitist attempt to berate my intelligence. To be honest, I was offended because he knew the historical facts about how ancient civilizations were destroyed and by whom. A topic that

I was too passionate about to really get into. As a challenge or further attempt to embarrass me, he pressed on.

"But seriously, why? And think carefully about your answer. If you can convince me of your position, then I will give you an A."

Now you know my dad didn't raise no suckers or cowards! I didn't get the nickname "Sister Souljah" for nothing.

"You mean to tell me that my grade will not be based upon the merits of my written essay, but rather if I can get you to see my point in changing American politics?" I asked with disgust.

"I already gave you a grade for your essay. The ORAL presentation of your argument is for Finals."

Needless to say, I accepted his challenge. It was time to teach him and everyone in the class who laughed at my expense, a valuable lesson; I could hold my own and I wasn't somebody to be played with!

I wanted to cripple him right away. I was taught that if you wanted to hurt a man, you attack his reputation, and the public will do the rest. Therefore, I needed to sway the class to my side of the argument immediately.

I hit him with a low blow coming out of the gate.

"First of all, with all due respect, Professor, one of the primary factors hindering our society from overcoming racism, is dying off with your generation. The archaic laws that support systemic and institutional injustices are changing, whether people such as you, like it or not," I said, matter-of-factly. Then I added, "This paradigm shift has two major factors: First, on a personal level, is the "diversity of love." People in my generation love who they love, and as you can see, that is looking very different than it did back in your day. Second, on a professional level, the focus has shifted to knowledge (which is different from education). Skill set is your earning power. Our generation is less concerned with race than with ability. I'm biracial, and the majority of my generational white counterparts (family members, friends, classmates, and colleagues) don't view race as the primary factor for us to coexist as equals."

He had a shelved look on his face but allowed me to continue uninterrupted.

"If I were the best programmer in the world, do you think Silicon Valley would care about my color? If I discovered the cure for cancer, do you think a white doctor or cancer patient would care about me being Black? We are not about holding people back from their greatness. If you're the best at what you do, I want you on my team. No matter your race, gender, ethnicity, social, economic, religious preference or affiliation."

"Ms. Washington, do you view me as a racist?" he asked in response.

Now, out of all the things I said, was this all he heard? It sounded like guilt to me, and I could smell blood in the water. A self-accusing spirit was the enemy of confidence. I saw a small decrease in arrogance after my insinuation.

I chuckled. "No, professor, while you say some outlandishly racist things from time to time, I view you more as an arrogant, ignorant person who has a strong disregard for other people's plights and suffrages. If I were a betting woman, I would bet that you are the descendant of slave owners and the very people who have robbed, raped, and exploited every race of people they encountered throughout time! But how I view you is not important. To be or not to be... a racist that is the question?" I punctuated my temporary advantage with a Shakespearian imitation.

It was my time to entertain now. Suddenly, the class appeared to be on my side, instigating things with "ooh's and aah's." I'd long since learned that no white person who isn't a racist wants to be viewed as one. It's the reason why nowadays everyone makes it a point to articulate, "Hey, you know me... I'm not racist." (Which may be true, but being ignorant or elitist isn't any better.)

I didn't quite witness the breakdown that I wanted. He was determined not to go down that easily.

"Interesting enough," he granted in response to my argument, pausing for effect. "While many generations of my grandfather's might be viewed as racist because they owned slaves, it doesn't mean that I'm racist," he said, almost convincingly.

He then added, "Why should a man like myself be held accountable for something people did whom I've never met?"

Now we're getting somewhere, I thought with pleasure. He made the typical mistake that most people make when debating uncomfortable issues. He personalized the accusations, rather than disputed the evidence. I took full advantage of the opportunity to represent myself, my father's teachings, and my generation.

"I don't hold their deeds against you. None of us are responsible for the actions of those who came before us. I would also bet that I'm the descendant of people who have done some horrible things as well. What's important and what we're individually responsible for as intelligent beings is CHANGE. Right now, right here, what are you doing to change the social injustices that exist today? That's what really matters.

"But you, like so many of your kind, you have benefitted so much, for so long, from things being the way they are that you're afraid of what change would look like for you and yours! In my opinion, you have disregarded my journey and have become desensitized towards the plight of people in my position. That's the only thing I can hold against you and those who share your views." I scolded him with the tongue of a millennial High Priestess.

"I can see your point of view," he relented with a hint of humility. "However, I can assure you that in my family, those ideologies went to the grave with my ancestors. I'm not like that. I would never teach my children or grandchildren that type of hatred. I detest and abhor those ignorant views," he insisted forcefully.

I wasn't quite ready to remove my stiletto from his ass. "But you still vote a straight Republican ballot, right?" I asked sarcastically, making the class laugh.

"Fair enough, fair enough..." I saw a devilish twinkle in his eye. "Would you have me vote straight Democrat?" he shot back, cleverly matching my sarcasm, though he received no support from the class.

"I think I told you, but I'll reiterate... I HATE AMERICAN POLITICS! I don't believe there should be gangs or gang leaders running for office! Party affiliations should be outlawed and placed on the domestic terrorism lists, along with Crips and Bloods; Vice Lords, and Gangster Disciples for destroying our democracy. Anyone running for office should be the best person for the job, and their ideas for social change must reflect the needs for the advancement of the American people. Not a party's agenda!" I preached from my soapbox, feeling like Winnie Mandela or Assata Shakur.

Amazingly, my entire class agreed with that point.

"Okay class, settle down," my professor implored, bringing a close to the spirited exchange.

"Thank you, Ms. Washington. It looks like, and I'm sure your classmates will agree, you won't be needing to attend Finals next week. But for the record, I'm not a racist and agree with almost everything you said."

You can't imagine the validation I felt, having stood toe to toe with a man far more educated and older than I, and won! Although I had often thought of him as an asshole, I had no real basis for the accusations of racism, other than the typical blindness associated with being removed from the culture. I simply challenged the idea that someone was "qualified" to dictate my reality to me, or somehow undermine my truth.

I think I actually felt a warrior's kind of respect for him after our debate. He could have easily backpedaled out of the conversation when things got hot, or used his position to accuse me of youthful arrogance, but he took his lumps, so to speak.

I soon came to learn that he hadn't just singled me out as I believed he had. As it turned out, each semester he selected one essay and allowed the student to give an oral presentation on the fly. Unbeknownst to the student, the result of the oral presentation was counted as their final grade. This moment was a prime example of me putting my lessons into practicality.

"Anger is a temporary state. You gotta be able to still think while you're angry and under pressure," my dad would say.

"Learn to channel your anger, and it becomes an asset. Anger fueled by ambition for resolution helps you to overcome challenges and obstacles. Every move gotta be your best move. So you gotta figure out how to move before you move, in order to win! When this process becomes second nature, you'll know you have arrived," he would preach.

But I still hate American Politics!

Now, let me take you on My Journey so you know how it all began....

Chapter Two:
Dad's Birthday Gift

I F I HAD TO choose from my past experiences, the single most life-altering event would have to be the moment that I realized my father was missing. As a young girl being raised in a loving, two-parent household, the extended absence of one parent doesn't go unnoticed for long. In fact, if not for his routine business trips (that's what we called them), I may have noticed a lot sooner than I did. Before I delve any deeper into the circumstances related to my dad's disappearance, I have to draw you a picture of my life until then.

I was born in Flint, Michigan, to Leroy and Kim Washington, on Wednesday, December 4, 1991 (on my dad's birthday). My parents had been high school sweethearts and very popular, due to their undeniable good looks. Both were biracial, with a mixture of Italian and African- American on my mother's side, and Korean and African-American on my dad's side. It doesn't take much imagination to visualize the attention they drew in the mid 1980s, when "lighter skinned" people were all the rage. My dad had more of a caramel complexion, with curly hair and slanted eyes.

In addition to being popular for their looks and outgoing personalities, they were also reputed to be trend setters when it came to fashion. They didn't just look the part; my parents were well known for showing up to social events like roller skating, high school dances, and sporting events.

Unlike most "pretty boys" in his age group, my dad was a tough guy who ran with a crew of troublemakers. If anyone was stupid enough to mistake the good looks for weakness, they soon learned the hard way not to judge a book by its cover. Sadly, my father suffered all too often for his "never back down" attitude.

As for me, I was the firstborn and treated like a princess. To say that I wanted for nothing would be an understatement. Between my parents, grandparents, aunts, and uncles (biological and extended), I probably suffered from a warped sense of reality. I had no knowledge of the cost of things, or what it meant to be unable to afford something. In fact, because of the financial stability prevalent in my family (from both sides of the law), I only noticed my good fortune by witnessing others' misfortune. This shocking revelation came later, after I was enrolled in school.

My charmed childhood also prevented me from suffering many of the early self-esteem issues common to girls my age. I can vividly remember darker-skinned girls being referred to as "black and ugly," even if they were pretty. Just being dark seemed to represent something unattractive, and I never understood why. The most I had to contend with was being asked what I was "mixed with," or being accused of thinking I was "all that." The fact that I was the product of attractive parents, with a mixture of at least three ethnicities, made me the exotic Black Girl. I didn't get called "white girl" or "black and ugly." My skin tone was caramel like my father's, enough not to be mistaken for white. That was enough to keep me happy.

This leads me to the single most devastating realization in my young life. It came as an unexpected revelation from a family friend. I had been awaiting my dad's return for quite some time. I remember asking my mom when he was coming home and being told that he said he loved me and not to worry.

At four years old, my curious mind wondered why his business trip had lasted longer than usual and would he bring me something special when he got home? Growing impatient, I asked every adult who came over to our house: "Have you seen my daddy?"

It must have been a painful experience for my mom to have to witness that. I can vividly remember the day when we went over a neighbor's house and I expected to see my dad there. As soon as we went inside, I asked about him.

"Is my dad here?" The look on the neighbor's face registered confusion.

"What makes you think your daddy would get out of jail and come here first? I'm sure he would want to see you before he saw me," she answered, stooping down to caress my face compassionately. She had no idea that she had put a dagger right through my little heart. Without knowing exactly how serious things were, I knew that jail was bad. I felt abandoned and afraid for my dad, all at once. Before I knew it, I was wailing and my mother was trying to console me. It was too late. I was beside myself with grief and my little body shook violently as I cried until my legs gave out and I collapsed in my mother's arms.

***

OF ALL THE THINGS I remember about my childhood and my dad, I vividly recall that he was supposed to take me for another ride on his motorcycle. He had recently, before his disappearance, put me on the front of the seat where I could hold the handlebars with him, and rode me around the corner. We probably never exceeded 15 mph, but to me, the noise from the engine made it feel like 100. He allowed me to believe that I was really driving the motorcycle, because my hands were next to his on the handlebars and his voice was in my ear.

"You wanna go faster, Pooh?"

"Yeah!" I giggled and revved the wrong part of the bars. My dad made speeding sounds with his mouth, while maintaining the same speed, but the effects worked. I felt like I was racing around the city with him behind me. I didn't want to ever ride in a car again!

By the time we had gone around the block twice, my mom was standing in front of the house, awaiting our return. I think she saw us the first time we passed the house but made it out too late to stop us from making another round. She ran out into the street as we approached the house.

"What are you doing with my baby?" she asked, angrily snatching me from the bike after my dad stopped. "Are you crazy? What if she had fallen off and gotten hurt?"

"You know I wasn't gonna do nothing to hurt my baby. Ain't that right Pooh?" my dad asked, reaching out to pinch my cheek.

"I wanna do it again!" I demanded excitedly.

I can remember the feeling of living dangerously with my dad on that motorcycle. It was a bonding moment, and till this day, I recall feeling like nothing could hurt me while I was with him. My mother was my idol, but my father was my hero. Nobody was tougher, richer, cooler, smarter, or more handsome. He looked at my mom and back at me, smiled, and winked at me.

"Your mama gonna jump on me if I let you race again today. I guess she thinks you're too little right now, but you're gonna be a big girl on your birthday when you turn five. We can race all over Flint then," he assured me, ignoring the scowl on my mom's face.

I beamed. "Can we race on my Granny's street too? I want everybody to see me!"

"As long as you take me with you. Not your mother, 'cause she be hating on us. Okay?" he teased my mom.

"Okay, Daddy! Just us. My mama don't like motorcycles. Do you, Mama?"

"Little girl, don't listen to your daddy," she said with a sneer. "I'm gonna show him a hater when he get in this house."

That was the last significant moment my father and I had spent together. The irony of learning that he was in jail was the fact that I felt angry, thinking that he might not be there on my birthday to let me race the motorcycle again. I was going to be a big girl and everyone was supposed to see us together. More than anything in this world, I wanted me and my dad to ride his motorcycle again.

Of course my birthday came and my dad wasn't there. I'm sure that he sent me the best gifts, but I can't remember. I have no memory of my fifth birthday party, but I remember the feeling of waking up without him in the house—a feeling that I would feel for decades, but never get used to.

Now, at thirty-one years of age, born on the same day, my father and I have an unexplainable closeness that transcends typical traits. We share a unique perspective on life and are kindred spirits. To say that I am his lifeline and he is my mentor doesn't quite articulate the depth of who "we" are. The fact that he has been incarcerated for twenty-seven years of my thirty-one years of living, and I haven't met any man who has had a deeper impact on my life, is a testament to his greatness. While being an incarcerated parent isn't ideal, being an absent parent is worse. I didn't suffer the tragedy of growing up, not knowing my father. My tragedy was having the greatest example of manhood, but unable to run and jump into his arms after school.

I missed out on having him run off all the little boys when we were adolescents. He never got to put the Band-Aids on my boo-boos when I skinned my knee. He didn't take me to buy my first car. (That's another story, altogether!)

Ultimately, he didn't give up on his parental responsibility, either. He has been a factor during every important moment in my life from day one. In fact, he has given me a special reason to pride myself on being shown a unique kind of love. I swear that I know women with fathers who live inside the home and do less than my dad. I've had numerous friends and family members say: "I wish that my dad was like yours. I love the way you guys interact." I am used to hearing it, but it still gives me pride.

So my reason for writing this book is to hopefully express to the world that there are positive effects possible even in negative situations. I am not attempting to project the shining example of American Success, as much as remarkable perseverance . . . the idea that love and dedication to maintaining the family unit can overcome many obstacles.

My story doesn't require me to embellish or omit. I can honestly express discontentment on one hand and superior reverence on the other. I can attribute my small accomplishments to the sage wisdom of a man who had a keen understanding of the pitfalls of the society that trapped him and who guided me through with patience and candor.

More importantly, I can offer insight into the struggle of young women who have similar experiences. Maybe fathers and daughters around the country will gain something from our story and become stronger because of it. However, if nothing else, I wanted to pay homage to someone who is one of a kind. I need my father to know that although the world has a habit of highlighting the shortcomings of fallen men, he is honored by the ones who matter.

For those of you who were hoping to read the autobiography of a rich and famous business mogul, stick around. By the end of the book, you may find that the journey is just as important as the destination. In fact, you will have a front row seat to history in the making. What better example of prosperity than a healthy family legacy? To my dad: If your advice and tutelage could be summed up in two words, they would be: "Man Up!"

To that, I reply: "Gladly!" I love you.

Chapter Three:

Where it All Began

2009 WAS A DYNAMIC year for me. I was seventeen years old, residing in Sandy Springs, Georgia, and living my best life. I had just finished my junior year at Sandy Springs High. I took comfort in knowing that all I had was one more year of school until all of my years of discipline and hard work would allow me and my crew to do it our way. Next was college and independence...at the same damn time!

I was especially excited to imagine my boyfriend Jay and I getting our first apartment together and starting our young lives, much like my mom and dad had. He was the love of my life and we already had almost three years under our belts, having met in my freshman year.

Jay wasn't just a handsome guy, with a great smile and cappuccino complexion; he was also one of my best friends. My girlfriends Aleysia, Neha, and Paris even liked us together. That much was obvious by the way they eventually stopped trying to get me to hang out with their boyfriends' friends.

My mother worked for one of the "Big Three" automotive companies, and she had been offered a promotion a while back. Something about a compensation package that included a move to the state of Texas. The subject had come up, but the implications of relocating were in such opposition to my life that I ignored the idea, hoping it would just go away.

As fate would have it, a few months later my mom had accepted the position and decided we were moving to Texas. Her second marriage to my little sister's father was ending in divorce, and she was excited about making a new start. It was arranged for me, my younger brother, and my sister to go with her. You can't imagine the shock and panic I felt when I heard the news. I experienced a kind of desperation I'd never felt before.

My life depended upon my finishing school, attending prom, and graduating with my crew. We had only been planning this course of events for half of my life (since the sixth grade)! I decided that I would literally do anything to stay. I even considered disappearing and trying to threaten my parents with rebellion. Not my best thinking, but I was DESPERATE! My young mind was hell bent on remaining in Georgia, and I used every tool in my teenage arsenal to convince my mom that dragging me to Texas would nearly kill me.

"All my friends are here...I'm almost done with school...You're ruining my life..." I pleaded my case. My mom wasn't hearing me.

She had no memory of her youth, when she'd made plans with no idea of how devastating it was when life unapologetically changed your plans. I even used my relationships with Paris, Neha, and Aleysia to try to gain some sympathy. I didn't dare mention my love life with Jay. She would have probably slapped me to the floor just for mentioning him. I could already hear the words before I hit the ground:

"You don't make no life-altering decisions for no boy at your age!"

Something in her makeup forced her to typically be harder on my sister and me than she was with my brother. In my opinion, she spoiled my brother to death and enabled him to do all the things that would come back to haunt him later in life.

To her credit, I was so adamant about my position that just when I thought I had worn her down, she hit me with a Floyd Mayweather right hand: "Let's just see what your father has to say about it." She'd decided to bring in back up.

I was devastated. That was a crushing blow to any hopes I had. I begged: "Please don't leave the decision to my father!" I was so desperate that I almost violated the unbreakable respect for our bond by uttering: "He hasn't been here since I was four." But even in my delirious mind, I knew better than to cross that line. Instead, I prepared myself to do battle with the no-nonsense, strict disciplinarian, Muslim man, who didn't allow anybody to outwit him. When my dad made a decision, it was as if the Pharaoh had spoken.

I didn't stand a chance, but my life depended on my at least putting up a fight. I realized that with him involved, I needed to come up with a plan B, and quick!

Just as I was thinking that I should probably get out of the house for a minute, in case he called, the phone rang and I saw the caller was him. I almost started crying right then. God had left me on stuck, I decided.

"Hey, Dad," I answered in our usual greeting. Only this time, dread muffled the excitement I usually felt when hearing his voice.

"Hey, baby!" He gave me his loving greeting in return.

My heart sank even further. This was my hero, and my life hung on his every word. I knew him well enough to know that he wasn't about to allow his only daughter to remain in Georgia, at seventeen years old, with no adult supervision.

Just like any attentive parent, hearing whatever nuances in my voice alerted him to my mood, he immediately asked, "What's wrong baby?"

My mother got right to it. "Is that your dad? Give me that damn phone," she demanded before I could soften him up with tears or whatever method I thought of. Instead of handing her the phone, I put it on speaker, trying to be slick. To be honest, I didn't want to hear what he had to say. It was obvious that he would have a million reasons why I couldn't stay, and that would be the end of that!

She apparently had informed my dad about the move months ago. I didn't recall he and I ever discussing the subject. I'm sure we did, but because I had no intention of leaving, I didn't remember whatever he said at the time. My mom was saying, "Well, your daughter doesn't want to move to Texas, so I told her I'd leave it up to you."

My eyes began to water immediately. I was sad and angry, but at the same time, I prepared myself to do battle. I knew it wouldn't be easy to wear him down or change his mind, but I had to try. My whole life depended on this conversation. It was MY life, after all.

I waited as my mother continued voicing her objections for what felt like an eternity, while my father listened. When she was done, my dad paused, apparently gathering his thoughts. I knew this was where my dreams died before I even got a chance to make my point. In his usual calm, cool, and collected manner, he said:

"Kim, you've done a great job of raising our kids. Pooh is responsible. She got her own car, a job, gets good grades, and you know she don't wanna leave that little boy down there," he began.

"That's what I'm afraid of. I don't want her getting pregnant or losing her way because I'm not down here," my mother said with concern.

I was still holding my breath, ready to argue for my independence. It only registered that I may have a little hope, when he said:

"Kim, our parents trusted us to spend the night and go out of town when we were that age, just so we wouldn't have to sneak around and lie to them." Then he dropped the bomb that made my heart start beating again.

"If we can't trust her in her senior year to be a young adult, how are we gonna trust her when she goes off to college next year?"

That was it! My father's decision was law. I had gotten my wish and didn't even have to say a word. *There is a God* was all that my naive ass could think. I almost jumped up and clicked my heels in excitement. I couldn't believe my luck.

Foolishly, I hadn't even considered that there would be stipulations. In the midst of my victory, I'd forgotten the rule that my dad had always reinforced about celebrating small victories as if they represented major success.

Of course the stipulations were strict, but they helped me to forge a relationship with my parents that has endured. That was my "welcome to adulthood" defining moment with my parents. Till this day I wonder if that whole episode was rehearsed and they spoke beforehand. It wouldn't be unheard of for parents as smart as mine.

I also learned a thing or two (or three) about Kim and LeRoy. One was: despite the fact that they were divorced, my mother still held a great deal of respect for my father. The feeling was apparently mutual. They had a bond built upon trust and shared a vision for parenting. Another thing I learned was that my mom was waaaayyy slicker than I gave her innocent character credit for! She was married to a former gangster, after all. She knew just what buttons to push and how to use my dad to bring out the best in me. It was no secret that I never wanted to disappoint him.

My mother knew that allowing him to stand up for me ensured that I would be much more responsible with my newfound independence and freedom. She was right, and I am forever in awe of how they made me a better version of myself by allowing me the chance to fail. I'd gotten an apparent double-dose of smarts somewhere in my genetic code from those two. It would be put to the test sooner than I imagined.

Chapter Four:
Jealousy Is the Worst of All Hates

I BELIEVE THERE COMES a time in every woman's life where she learns something about herself that enhances her self-confidence permanently. It's almost like learning that you've had an untapped superpower hidden inside yourself all along. You somehow go from reluctantly dealing with issues, to "Bitch Try Me!" The sad part is that it typically gets revealed during a tragic moment in your life.

Having succeeded in forging the first stages of my newfound independence by convincing my parents to allow me to stay in Georgia, I was a seventeen-year-old living on Cloud 9. I quickly moved in with my best friend Ley (Aleysia), who was a grade behind me, her mom Drea, and her older sister Taj, who attended Georgia State University. I swear, we had all kinds of Black Girl Magic going on in that cramped three-bedroom apartment.

Ley and I shared a room, which was perfect because we had been best friends and sisters since middle school. Plus, her sister Taj was a few years older and doing her own thing, for the most part. We

31

were all like sisters, but Ley and I were like the Wonder Twins. We even looked alike.

As part of the arrangement that allowed me to remain in Georgia while my mom relocated to Texas, she and my dad assisted me with finances. I had a job at a Chuck E. Cheese, my own car, and was doing well in school, so my parents rewarded my efforts by ensuring that I could be comfortable enough to enjoy being young, without being babied. Thus, my father (from prison in Michigan) sent Drea $500 per month for allowing me to live in her home, and my mom sent me an allowance to help cover things like gas, phone bill, and incidentals. My job at Chuck E. Cheese made it possible to pay my insurance, do some shopping, and keep a few dollars for activities. Despite the constant jokes, I wasn't the least bit embarrassed by my workplace. I didn't expect to be there long-term, but for the moment, it fit perfectly into my model for independence.

My daily life consisted of Ley, my boyfriend Jay, school, work, and trying to be the flyest chick around. At that age, you tried hard to set yourself apart from others in your peer group by dressing with a unique flair and being seen in a crowd of people on the same level. Even then, Ley and I would plan our future takeover of the world by first dressing like the starlets we saw on reality TV. If you planned to be a boss, you had to look like one, right?

I remember watching the award shows to see what Rihanna, Beyoncé, and Kim Kardashian were wearing. We imagined that we looked as good as they did. We just needed to find our own hustles. Writing, acting, modeling, and music were some of the things that we dabbled in, hoping to get a lucky break.

The truth of the matter is, I had come from a long line of overachievers. So I thought none of my friends felt the pressure to succeed more than I did. I had cousins who played professional football. I had great-aunts and -uncles who were politicians back in Flint, Michigan, where I was born. Even my parents were the topic of discussion at family reunions and other functions for all the things they had done together.

People always reminded me of how much I looked like him. It was a given that any time his name came up, there was a story to be told. I loved that the story of my parents being high school sweethearts got told over and over. It was almost like Beauty and the Beast because my dad was an intelligent hoodlum and my mom was the beauty. I imagined that for myself and Jay.

Aside from the pressure I felt to make a mark in this world, I craved my own identity. I needed to carry the torch and leave a legacy like my dad had. I mean, this man had been incarcerated since I was four years old, but his presence had never been diminished. If he spoke, people listened. I can recall a few times when he had to scold me verbally, and it felt like he had whipped me. He was just that kind of man. If there was anything that he couldn't do, I hadn't figured it out yet. As his firstborn, I wanted to be the female version of the man whose voice made the world move.

***

AT THE TIME, I was living a charmed life, I must say. In fact, I had become so comfortable with the stability of my protective cocoon that I was more than blindsided by the abrupt way things changed for me. In retrospect, there were subtle clues that should have hinted at the underlying feelings held against me, but some things can only be taught by life's greatest professor...experience!

It was an ordinary day. I had just finished getting dressed for work, after taking a shower. I was thinking to myself that I was cutting it close by trying to make the fifteen-minute drive in heavy rain. My shift started in about twenty-five minutes, and I was slow-poking.

"Lauren, I need you to go pick up Taj from work. I ain't going out in this weather," Drea said with a tone of authority. Any other time it would have been no problem. I wouldn't have even been tripping on her commanding me to do her job, but today was the wrong day for a number of reasons. First, I was running late and had already had two warnings. I had been warned that the next time would have consequences. I really didn't want to have to find another job when I had things worked out perfectly already. Showing up late again guaranteed that I would be fired. Second, it was Drea's responsibility to pick up Taj. It hadn't just started raining suddenly. She could have asked me a lot earlier, but had chosen not to. It reminded me of my dad saying: "A failure to plan on your part doesn't constitute an emergency on my end."

The fact was that Taj was like my sister, and I would never intentionally leave her hanging, but I wasn't even given the courtesy of being asked if I could do it. That pissed me off.

Even though I realistically couldn't make it, my mind searched for alternatives, because I felt obligated to appease the woman who had opened her home to me. My options were to try to speed to Taj's job, pick her up and let her drop me off at work and keep the car until it was time for my shift to end...or...I could just pick her up, drop her at home, and possibly lose my job...or I could let them figure it out themselves. They were adult women.

The first option was a no-go. My parents had expressly forbidden me to let anyone use my car due to insurance and lawsuit implications. I couldn't betray their trust. Option two threatened to disrupt my independence when I lost my job. Drea would surely have something to say about that. She could be overly critical of me at times. It seemed that she sometimes considered me an outsider or third-wheel in her and her daughters' lives.

Granted, Ley and I shared an apparently unbreakable bond, due to being closer in age and interests, but she and Taj were both my sisters. After a couple months of me living with them, Drea would sometimes say little things that hurt my feelings. Things like "we" don't do "this or that" in this house. Or she would try to drive a wedge between me and Ley, by comparing us or saying that I thought I was special.

As a guest, I expected there to be some uncomfortable adjustments, so I ignored my bruised feelings or talked to Ley about them. She always had my back. She would say that I was brought up differently, and her mother didn't want her and Taj to expect to be treated like me. Whatever that meant.

I didn't really understand the thought process behind her opinions of me. I considered that it was possibly because of my father being such a huge presence in my life from prison, while she was forced to be a single parent. It was no secret that my dad had been a heavyweight hustler and convicted of murder on two occasions. Maybe she thought of me as some privileged mob daughter. Nothing could have been further from the truth. My dad had renewed his faith in Islam, earned college degrees, and given me the kind of discipline and guidance that made his former life seem like a fairytale.

I also reasoned that people were often offended by what seemed to obligate them to you. Did the monthly payments from my dad make Drea feel hesitant to express her act of generosity? Or prevent her from weaponizing her benevolence? Did she want more money? I wasn't sure. All I knew was that she became less and less considerate of my feelings over time.

Neither Drea nor Ley knew it, but it affected my self-esteem a little to hear criticism about my choice of clothing or my looks. I sometimes wondered if being pretty relegated me to negative vibes from women. In my mind I was just Lauren, the loyal "ride or die" friend. We were all pretty girls, but I noticed the flippant remarks about my "yellow ass" or "thinks she too cute." I repeatedly brushed it off as cultural growing pains. In the Black community, older women often spoke rudely to keep younger women "in their place." It was like hazing in college. A rite of passage. Not that I could ever see myself treating people that way.

Drea was the one who had always been on me about being more responsible and constantly called me a spoiled brat. I worked at Chuck E. Cheese for peanuts and was fortunate that my parents helped with an allowance. Where were the Mercedes and butler that she seemed to imagine?

"I'm running late for work myself," I explained to Drea, expecting her to understand. As rude as she had been, I was willing to find any reasonable compromise. That is just who I am as a person. It had reached the point where the facts had to be laid out. I knew that Ley could feel the tension and I didn't need to drag it any further.

"I can see that you don't know how things go around here. You ain't a team player, and if you don't go get your sister, you're gonna have to find somewhere else to stay!"

Drea's words cut through my rational approach and immediately angered me. I was not brought up to disrespect my elders at any cost. I especially wouldn't be rude to my best friend's mom, but I hadn't been taught to be weak and cower when abused either. I had to draw the line. I wasn't about to let anyone speak to me as if I were a peon with no choice but to submit. I ignored the sting of betrayal and held my composure.

"Well, I'm on my way to work. I won't have a job if I'm late. Taj just got off work. She can find her own way home. And if it's okay with you, I'll come pick up my stuff once I finish my shift," I replied with restrained anger as I walked toward the door.

My best friend was crying, and my heart broke with every step that got me closer to the door. I prayed that Drea would stop me before I made it outside the apartment and dismiss the whole thing as foolish. I loved these people as if we shared the same blood. It couldn't have come to this over something that wasn't my fault, I told myself.

"Fine by me," Drea fired back as the door shut behind me.

There may have been a possible chance for reconciliation in her mind, but not in mine. I didn't have time for her mess. I would have to figure it out later, because I needed to get to work on time. Although I expected to be emotional over the whole episode, amazingly I didn't shed a single tear. Maybe it was something in the way I rationalized the entire thing from the start that gave me confidence in my decision. There was nothing more I could have done to avoid this ending. I was forced to stand on that and I had no regrets.

Drea had tried to force me to pick up Taj, when she could have done so herself. She then threatened to make me leave her home, rather than to compromise. That was extreme, to say the least and hinted at something deeper. Maybe it was a form of envy. The worst part about someone who may be jealous or envious of you is that you never know the reasons. Yet it shows itself at the slightest provocation.

I assume that there comes a moment in every girl's life when she realizes that she's deserving of respect and won't allow anyone to disregard her. This was my moment. In retrospect, I actually feel good about my display of character. I wasn't homeless or destitute. I hadn't been insensitive or arrogant while living with them. In fact, I had been grateful and content. That made the unwarranted disregard for my emotions even more devastating.

***

I MADE THE CALL to my mom, who was very angry, but reserved enough not to speak badly of Drea. Instead, she taught me a lesson about the value of relationships. She called my aunt Monique (her best friend from high school), who didn't hesitate to invite me to stay with her and my cousin Pooter in Atlanta. That was the kind of juice my parents had. I had witnessed them both call in favors from people who were happy to assist. This was evidence of some magic formula that they shared. I understood why they had been a power couple at one time. Moving in with my aunt turned out to be a way better situation for me. As my dad says, "We plan and God plans. He's a way better planner than we are."

My little cousin Pooter and I got along well. While she was ten years younger than me, the living situation was conducive to my being a senior in high school. I quickly made the adjustment due to the warm reception and my aunt's respect for my maturity. She allowed me to spend my final year of high school learning what it would be like to have total independence when I started college next year.

I saw Ley in school, and she seemed like she had been brainwashed into believing that I was in the wrong. In fact, she went as far as to act like she wanted to fight about it. When I tried to express my side, she didn't want to hear it. This wasn't the sister I had known since middle school.

I wanted to believe that she was just hurt about my not being there and couldn't accuse her mom, but I was truly like f#@k her as well, if she felt like that! I had done all the ass-kissing I was going to do. The new Lauren had learned a valuable lesson about standing on principle. Not only had my parents been proud of me, but the universe had given me a better environment as a reward.

This situation served as the first major incident where I felt the unforgettable sting of abandonment and betrayal. My relationship with Ley was ruined. The one person I could call my "day one" or my "ride or die" had not ridden with me, and our sisterhood had died. It tore at my heart like nothing I had ever experienced at that point, and the sad part was that I couldn't run to my best friend about how I felt.

I also couldn't be as trifling as to speak badly about her to people who noticed the distance and tried to act as though they were concerned. I wondered why she thought that slandering my name would make her look better. Didn't she know that her fake friends hated us equally? She could be dumb enough to play the game like that, but my shoes had been tied by real ones, I reminded myself. To call her my sister and then trash her to outsiders would be a mark on my character. In the end, I just swallowed my pain and flipped my hair. Instead of taking over the world with Ley, I would just have to do it alone and show her what Lauren Washington was made of. She had chosen to forsake a legacy and throw away years of loyalty. I took that hard, but it made me stronger.

The years went by, life went on, and I was glad that my dad had prepared me to invest heavily into myself. That girl in the mirror would sometimes be the only one to believe in the power of perseverance. I didn't hate the game or the players. I just carved my own niche and did me...to the fullest!

Chapter Five:

Jay

I MET MY FIRST love, Jay, during freshman year at North Springs High School. We were in the same third-hour civics class, and he hung out with a guy my friend liked. We seemed to keep being in the same places and ended up exchanging numbers. He had his own unique swagger that I thought was cute.

Jay had the quintessential good looks of a male model. Over six feet, tatted sleeve on his right arm, jet black curly hair, goatee, and heavy brows that made him look Puerto Rican. His look was pretty boy meets bad boy. He was always dressed to impress and the kind of guy who could have a good time at a six-year-old's birthday party.

He played sports and was into cars and fashion. He had a rugged edge, but he wasn't a thug. Those things attracted me, and discovering that we had other things in common drew us very close. We were both young, but he displayed a mature dedication in the things he did. He was different from most of the dudes who tried to push up on me. For one, he didn't come across as thirsty or childish.

Looking back, he didn't actually shoot his shot as much as just showed his worth.

I took comfort in the fact that my mom liked him also. Well...as much as a mother could like a guy who was interested in her young daughter. I couldn't tell if my dad liked him, but Jay was respectful and that's all that mattered at that time. My father had only spoken to him over the phone a few times. I didn't ask, but I'm sure that he simply informed Jay that I was his Princess, and if he did anything to violate me, I had brothers and cousins who would break his legs (or something equally effective). I was just happy that my father didn't express a strong dislike for him, because his opinion was like the gospel to me.

As you might be able to imagine, senior prom was coming, and for a young girl in love, that was almost like planning for a wedding. The dress, coordinating colors with my boyfriend, the limo and hotel room for the events afterwards, had to all be perfectly executed. Planning prom was not just a big thing for me; this was the highlight of my life!

Not only was I in love, but this occasion represented my opportunity to shine one last time before leaving for greener pastures. A prom challenged everyone to try to outdo one another and leave your name in the history books at your school. If we were elected King and Queen, you'd never hear the end of that, I imagined.

At this time in my life, splurging with a big budget was out the question for me. Of course my dad came through with his end, but over the years I had perfected getting by with less. I had become the Queen of being "fly" on a budget. I'd already decided that I wanted to wear something different than the traditional store-bought dress. In fact, I wanted to add some flair to my appearance and pay homage to my Asian heritage. I loved setting myself apart. I took a chance by purchasing some fabric online that I brought to a seamstress to have tailored according to my design vision. I was nervous about the risk of it not coming out right, but I ended up being very happy with the outcome. Nobody came close to having a dress like mine.

That night, I showed up and got so many compliments that I felt like a celebrity. Everybody wished that they had thought to design their own dress and even asked me if I could do designs for them. I basked in all the attention I received at my senior prom, and I didn't care if I was Prom Queen or not, after the reception I received. That minor victory validated my creative process and gave me the confidence to expand that gift into other areas of my life.

I still find it amazing how the unexpected things had such a huge impact on my self-esteem and confidence level. I had always been different, so I was used to the gift and the curse of my looks. I knew that I would never have the privilege of being "average." Obviously my multicultural background made me the center of attention, a lot. It wasn't always positive, but it wasn't always negative either. It was a blessing that my parents and a number of family members had lived with the same conditions and prepared me for them.

For example, my relatives on my dad's side of the family were Korean and Black, while my mom's side were Black and White. Thus, our views on racism were typically compounded. Too dark for the European mindset, too bright to be considered "Black Black." I often wondered how people could think of my experience as less real? I have always been undeniably Black, but what if I had wanted to be undeniably any of my other ethnicities? Would that affect the person I was on the inside? These were some of the things that Jay and I openly discussed. His light complexion and my own skin seemed to represent balance to me. He was there for me through all the growing pains, and I couldn't imagine life without that dynamic.

Prom was the last hurrah before we graduated and got down to the "grownup" things that we had planned. Our careers were 75% decided, but there was always the possibility that the world would wake up and learn that we had taken the shortcut to super-stardom. I'm just saying...

***

ONE MONTH LATER, I walked across the stage at Sandy Springs High School to receive my diploma with the biggest smile ever. It was finally over! Everybody was there celebrating me. It felt so good to once again be the center of attention and one step closer to being somebody in this world.

I was really just happy to be done with school and anxious for the next step in my plans for world domination. I guess you could say that I was RUNNING towards my destiny and the future couldn't come fast enough. In that moment, I realized the value of what my dad always said: "Every milestone should be recognized, but graduating is nothing to celebrate." This was just another accomplishment that moved me closer to the ultimate goal. Not an ending, but another beginning.

My dad's position was that I was supposed to do well in school and get good grades.

"Pooh, we have so much more to accomplish!" He often reminded me to remain sober. "No athlete is satisfied with just winning his first game when he's focused on a championship. Anything less is just part of a journey. Only losers celebrate every small accomplishment because they ain't used to winning."

My dad would teach me the hardest lessons in the middle of any premature victory dance. Sometimes I would think that he was too serious about life and wondered why he couldn't just enjoy the moment.

Later in life, those conversations would become invaluable. This man understood emphatically what life had in store for someone who took their eye off the ultimate goal. His constantly preaching "focus and preparation" came in handy in all aspects of my life as I took the journey into womanhood.

***

IMMEDIATELY FOLLOWING MY GRADUATION ceremony, my parents planned a beautiful Open House for me. They rented a party room at Dave & Buster's, just north of Atlanta, to host it. It was decorated with all kinds of banners and balloons and crowded with people celebrating me. All my family and friends were there to basically recap my life's accomplishments and encourage me to reach for the stars. This night was truly a celebration, and I had no worries that my dad would remind me of the work left to do.

It was truly a heartfelt, genuine moment, and I felt validated for the work that I had put in. I knew more than a few girls who had gotten pregnant, or dropped out of school to pursue a career in music videos, or were stripping, scamming, or doing other things that seemed to only offer immediate gratification and short-term rewards.

Lord knows that I had sometimes considered the temptation of quick money schemes when my cash was low or I wanted to feel accomplished sooner than later. So in that respect, I was glad to be seen for my sacrifices as well. People didn't hesitate to express their expectations for my extraordinary future. I was LeRoy and Kim's daughter, after all.

Because of that, dozens of people with whom I didn't have relationships showed up and gave me lots of money and gifts. People really went the extra mile to put on for me, and I appreciated that. Many did so on the strength of my dad, and I never stop being amazed by that fact. They say it takes a village to raise a child. I'm living proof of that.

I'd like to offer a very sincere "thank you" for all the times his friends have generously helped my dad and me accomplish our goals.

***

THE MOST MEMORABLE PART of my Open House came when my dad's cousin C.C. (Carolyn) stood up to address me. C.C. said some nice things to express her being proud of me and ended her speech with: "Last, but not least, I have a letter from LeRoy that he wanted me to read to Lauren." It caught me off guard, and I was really excited for my dad's presence to be in the room with me. Everyone was silent as she began reading.

In the name of Allah. The most Gracious. The most Merciful.

My Dearest Darling Daughter,

I'm so proud of you for this great accomplishment! I thank God and your mother for the wonderful gift that I have received in you. You are my brightest star and if I could use one word to describe you, it would be "aesthetic." Your character exemplifies the true essence of beauty. It worries me at times, how fast you've grown up to become this beautiful young lady and saddens me that I can't be there with you. Knowing this, it is terribly difficult at times for me to be at peace within. However, I have learned over the years that the furrows and ridges of inconsistency and pain are the contours that gives life its meaning. I can rage at the Heavens for separating us, but I must simultaneously thank them for the blessed gifts that I have been given in YOU!

Should anyone ask me what is my contribution to the world, I can say that my conscience rests joyously with the knowledge that I had a hand in bringing you into it. You are my greatest offering. So live up to that honor.

With that being said, I want to give you some words of wisdom to carry with you on this journey. Where much is given, much is expected in return. And God has given you many gifts.

Develop, cherish, and use your talents wisely.

You have the ability to create the world that you want to live in. Nothing is fixed for you. You can conquer anything you put your mind to! Knots can be untied, chains can be broken, walls can be smashed down, and doors can be pushed open. So keep that self-determination and confidence in your abilities. I love that distinctive quality about you.

Always listen to your inner voice and never let others drown it out. Measure your words and balance your works with your gifts carefully. Let NO one define who you are! Some will deify you and treat you like a princess, while others will want to dismiss you as a peasant. Some will embrace you, others will shun you. This is the world we live in, but their opinions of you will not increase or diminish the value of who you truly are!

Allow none to tempt you to abandon your principles. Always follow what is right. Stick to the path of honesty and integrity. You are a strong young lady and let nothing break you.

I'm soooo proud of you....

You are my blessed gift from God. Now I introduce you to the World! And the World to You! So remember:

Proper Preparation Prevents Poor Performance!

If not now, then when? If not you, then who?

Live Well, My Love.

Be good, and if you can't be good, then be safe.

The World is Now Yours & The Best is Yet to Come!

I Love You With All My Heart!

You are Me and I am You! ~

Love Always

Your Father,

Dad

I cried all the while my dad's letter was being read. The tears flowed so hard that they ruined my makeup. I could hear his voice as if he was standing next to me. He always thought of everything. I felt a huge sense of pride as I realized that I loved this man, not just because he was my father. I loved him because he had done his job very well. He hadn't shirked his responsibility simply because he lived on another planet or because my mom was no longer his wife. This man had unwittingly (or very deliberately) given me the example of the character traits I would need in my future husband. I didn't have to search to find my first example of manhood, because I had been raised with one in my life.

I would never answer my phone again with fear of my dad reminding me of the work "we" still had to do. In fact, I welcomed it. All along I had viewed my dad's lessons as loving criticisms, when in actuality they were the secret language between twin souls. No different than the Warrior who teaches his daughter Kung Fu in the movies. He had been giving his firstborn daughter all the tools necessary to do battle with the world. "You are me and I am you..." I had been saying it all along, but the meaning had taken on a new clarity in the moment.

It occurred to me at that moment that 90% of things you experience in life boil down to perspective. Tragedy often becomes the basis for comedy. What makes you laugh will often make you cry as well. The struggle is the biggest part of the triumph. It's all dependent upon how you see it. J.C. Williams summarizes the concept with: "If you're in Hell and you love it...you're actually in Heaven...and vice-versa."

Though I remember my dad's letter word for word, I still go back and read it from time to time. It still makes me cry and it still leaves me in awe at how, true to form, he still managed to subtly remind me of the moment being a minor step in the long walk of life. It seems that when I look back, I regard that celebration as the moment that my shoes had been officially tied. I was ready to walk into womanhood and exceed even the lofty expectations of those who were my support system. If anyone thought that Little Lauren would settle for mediocrity, they were sadly mistaken. All I had to do now was EVERYTHING!

Chapter Six:
Moving to Texas

MY MOTHER AND FATHER were very family oriented. When you hear the stories about my father, you notice that one of his standout characteristics was that he is all about the family. Back in the day, he and my uncles would hit the streets, hustling all day, then meet up at either my mom's, my aunt Amy's, or occasionally my Granny's, to feed all the kids. It was like a holiday dinner every day.

After my sophomore year in college, I decided that I wanted to transfer to Texas to be closer to Mama and my siblings, Bruh and Maddy. Jay wanted to leave Atlanta too. It's ironic that as young adults we fight all those years to find our independence, only to learn that there is nothing like being around family. At the time, General Motors was hiring third-generation workers. Mama told the entire family she could get everyone in. To most of our family, a job working at GM sounded like the California gold rush. We knew that a good portion of our clan was headed to Texas.

Jay and I arrived first. No sooner had we gotten there than many of my family members appeared as well. My mother's house was the hub. Mama tentatively gave everybody a two-check grace period, before we all had to get our own places. That grace period usually turned into months.

My cousins came from far and wide—Nukie from Tennessee, Jerome from Ohio, and Kiesha from Flint. The house was bursting at the seams with people, but we were too busy having fun to notice, most of the time. The following year, my Granny came after Paw Paw passed away. She became a permanent fixture at my mother's house. It almost felt like we'd had a family reunion in Texas and everyone decided to stay. We literally had four generations under one roof at some periods.

Next my aunt Amy and her significant other came with their youngest children. They were real grownups, so they had their own housing situation arranged before they showed up.

When Kiesha arrived, I felt like I finally had somebody with whom I could relate. The men in the family were getting on my nerves with their antics. You know how men like to try to mark their territory? Especially in a new environment. With her around, there was finally some estrogen to counteract all the testosterone in the air.

Keisha was truly my saving grace. She was a few years older than me, and also very beautiful and classy. She resembled a top video vixen. She was definitely thick in all the right places, with a medium brown complexion, big doe eyes, pouty lips, and elegant demeanor. She looked like the pretty girl who could drag a chick if they tried her. She had a sweet disposition, but still had that Flintstone edge. (She certainly got an honest dose of whatever was in that Flint water growing up.) She was always ready to kick some ass if she had to. And I had her back! I had only seen Kiesha one time since we moved to Atlanta, but it was like we had never separated. It was crazy how we still had so much in common. We were thick as thieves.

Chapter Seven:

Keisha

EVERYONE HAS THAT ONE person in their life who knows you better than anyone else. All of your deepest and darkest secrets. The good and the bad. Your strengths and your weaknesses. Your fears and your desires. What drives you and what makes you SHUT DOWN! Someone who has been there for you through thick and thin, even though you didn't necessarily deserve it. That one person you didn't always treat as well as you should have and they still had your back, regardless.

If you don't have a person like that in your life, then I feel sorry for you. It's a priceless feeling and also humbling to know that someone could love you so selflessly. For me, that person has been my cousin Kiesha. We are only a few years apart, but she's wise beyond her years. My father says it's because she pays attention to details (I can't wait till he says that about me). Kiesha is smart and beautiful, but what I admire most about her is the humility and loyalty she displays. Those are some of the rarest qualities on Earth. Especially difficult to find in the same person.

While she comes from humble beginnings, she has never displayed an ounce of jealousy or coveted anything that anyone else may have had. Actually, she's the furthest thing from a hater that a woman can be. I guess we take after our fathers in that respect. My dad tells us all the time, "I don't want another man's money, belongings, woman, or problems. I want my own!"

She is also one of the strongest people I know. She just has that tenacity and innermost fortitude that makes those around her feel like "we got this." Her mother recently passed away, in early 2023, and I don't think I could have remained as composed as she was. I have no doubt that her pain was unbearable, but she elected to channel the grief into embracing family even harder.

She reminded me of the stories I heard about her father, my uncle Luke. My dad's brother Luke passed away in the late 80s; before either Kiesha or I were born (her mom was pregnant with her). Luke was the first leader of my father's band of brothers, which was made up of cousins and blood brothers. In the Black family, first cousins might as well be considered siblings. At least, that's the way my father's generation was raised. My uncle Luke, his brother Uncle Lester, and my dad all have children by my mother and her two sisters, making our family double-related!

My dad and all his brothers looked up to my uncle Luke. He wasn't a massive man in stature, more like my dad's size. I guess being smaller men; they had to be tougher than the rest. But I suppose it helps that the rest of my uncles and cousins were bigger guys and tough as well. Like my dad, Luke's reputation of being a handsome, smart, stomp-down hustler and ladies' man preceded him. But his most memorable trait was teaching his brothers to be loyal to each other. Kiesha definitely inherited that trait from her dad.

Neither most of my uncles, my mom, nor her sisters talk much about Uncle Luke, I suppose due to the pain associated with his loss and HOW our family lost him. My dad, on the other hand, talks to Kiesha and me quite often about the lessons he learned from her dad: "In the end, family is all you got, and the family you build is the only family you'll have. Being blood don't make us family. It just makes us related!"

This was Uncle Luke's philosophy and one of the principles that my dad would come to live by. My dad and my uncle June were in prison when Luke was killed. Both of my grandmothers and great aunts say that they thank God for that!

Everyone says that Uncle Luke was a smooth operator, but my dad has always been a hothead. There was no telling what kind of domino effect his brother's death would have caused if my dad had been home. All of his other brothers and cousins were sure to have followed my dad into battle. Or they would have possibly been together when Uncle Luke's death occurred, and our family would have lost more than one member.

It's apparent that Kiesha and I got some of our "family oriented" traits genetically from our fathers. To say that we got it honestly would be putting it mildly. Our fathers are brothers and our mothers are sisters. (Doesn't that make us more sisters than cousins? Hmmm...) We've never been gangsters or criminals, but I know we get our Hustler's Ambitions from them for sure! (Kiesha might have even inherited a little bit of their gangster because she ain't no punk. Don't even think to try her!) Even when we're not on the same hustle, she's been my coach and biggest supporter, and pushes me to be the best version of myself in all my endeavors. She also keeps me grounded.

My entrepreneurial spirit makes me brazen and a risk-taker. I subscribe to the "bigger risk, bigger gain" ideology. Kiesha is more reserved. The "What about the bills that are due tomorrow?" type. In this respect, we balance one another. Our common denominator is that we are both completely dedicated to leveling up and getting our piece of the American Dream. Our ultimate goal is to obtain financial family success, much like our fathers had, but by utilizing an approach that will allow us to keep our wealth, our health, and our freedom. We've tried our hand at numerous business endeavors, from making and selling candles, to forming and sustaining a nationwide nonprofit, and thirty ventures in between.

Some ideas worked and some failed. All in all, the comfort of having someone to strive with and know you can trust has mattered more than any financial success alone. My "ride or die" has never abandoned me in my time of need, and I can only hope to be to her, what she has been to me! Girl, I will always have your back, and as BMF's Flenory brothers, Meech and Terry, would say: "From the womb to the tomb . . . we are related and loyal to each other, to death do us part!"

Kiesh, we don't have the same parents, but we just ought to. My mom and dad love you as if you were their own daughter. You're truly the only person I don't mind sharing my parents with. It makes me proud when you acknowledge that my dad has been a great influence in your life. That's a constant reminder of the lessons we've learned from him, together, over the years. It amazes me how you can so easily become like my right arm. Like when my dad calls, you will automatically get a pen and paper ready. I'll be like "Girl, you about to take notes?" You'll answer: "... and you're not?" I especially like that I'll forget something and you'll be like: "Remember what Uncle L said" and pull out your notepad.

I guess my dad's observations are accurate. Kiesha does pay attention to details. More impressively, there are times when she doesn't have the solution to the problems I have, but is quick to remind me of a source that is always at our disposal: "What do you think Uncle L would say?" Or maybe: "We should wait for him to call." That makes me smile inside, knowing that she sees what I see and really loves her uncle.

Girl, you are my rock! I love me some you and thank you for all that you bring to my life. You keep me grounded in my truest nature and encourage me to be myself at all times. Your wisdom has prevented me from tainting my blessings and made me a better person. Most of all, thank you for loving me with all my flaws.

In case I haven't told you lately: "I love you, Big Sis. You're one of my Sheroes!"

And as your Uncle L would say: "The best is yet to come!"

Chapter Eight:

GM

GENERAL MOTORS THIRD-GENERATION workers seemed like third-generation slaves to me. I guess I get that mentality from my father. He understood working for the company to be a necessary evil for our families to prosper, but he didn't like it one bit.

My grandparents on both sides—Paw Paw and Granny, and Grandpa Washington (T-Roy) and Granny Deb—all started in the factory back in the late 60s and early 70s. Each of them retired from that same slave plantation.

My mother was a second-generationer and the first of her sisters to start working in the plant. I could relate to my father's feelings firsthand. I hated seeing my mother come home too exhausted to do anything with us. She got up for work at 4 a.m. and crawled back into the bed by 7 p.m., only to repeat the cycle daily. On the weekends all she wanted to do was rest, so she could go back to the plantation on Monday. She knew it was stealing the best portion of her life, but what could she do? She had three kids to feed and raise, on her own, with very little outside help.

At least it gave her some independence and us some stability. She didn't seek out welfare or walk around with her hand out, expecting something to fall into her lap because she was pretty. I now see similarities in our strength and determination. She made it possible for me to escape the same fate, and I thoroughly respect what she sacrificed for us. Too often the offspring of hard-working parents get the accolades for their apparent success, without crediting those who made the transition possible.

Even my father said that it didn't start to bother him that his father and stepmother worked so hard in that factory, until he became a conscious man. He witnessed all those years of servitude, seeing his father come home with his entire body sore, head to toe. Sometimes he was too tired to even take off his smelly work uniform. He would just stumble into the house and fall asleep on the living room floor. And for what? To make that corporation the number one company in the world? I guarantee you that not a single retiree could approach the president of GM and borrow $5. Not a single corporate executive could say with any certainty that he recognized one line worker in my family that slaved for thirty-five years making them wealthy.

To add insult to injury, they didn't even give their best slaves a damn Cadillac upon retirement! You could spend your entire life building a car that you would never own. I think they call that "satirical irony."

My dad made a strong point when he said that because of that experience, he vowed to never work that hard to make someone else rich. While I'm grateful for the General Motors Corporation and what my people built while being employed there, working there just wasn't for me either. Two weeks in, I got into it with a supervisor and got fired. At that time, it was the best thing that could have ever happened. As my dad likes to say: "Adversity builds character." I was soon to become a living testament to that. By then, I had already worked short stints at a couple of jobs and failed at a few business ventures of my own. I knew way back then that I didn't want to work for nobody! That meant that at this point, I had to sink or swim. Or as my grandfather would say: "Shit, piss, or get off the pot." I've been self-employed ever since.

That negative experience of the supervisor overstepping the boundaries of respect and expecting me to be a good little monkey, only reinforced the values that my father had been teaching me all along. Workers are meant to remain just that...workers! Being employed by another comes with a built-in ceiling. I needed a way to fly as high as I could, or fall down and break something trying to fly. It was no different than when I was in high school and wanted to be a model. My dad said: "Pooh, modeling is cool as long as you're doing it to learn the 'in's and out's' of the business. But why just be a model when you can own a modeling agency?" Likewise, when I worked at Chuck E. Cheese, he asked if the company made a lot of money. When I answered yes, he said, "Let's buy one then!" He beat into my head that I had no excuse to not achieve greatness.

At the time I was too young to understand the concept he was teaching me. I used to think of my financial future in terms of a better hourly wage, overlooking numerous other possible means of enrichment. Like being paid by the day, or by the project. I now consider that some wealthy people may only get paid every few months, but the scores are substantial.

It was around this time that my father had me read this book: *Rich Dad, Poor Dad* by Robert Kiosaki. It was then that the lightbulb clicked on in my head. Subscribing to this very same mentality was why my father had money! He inherited the spirit from my grandmother. My Granny immigrated to America from Korea in the 60s, unable to speak a bit of English. But through the ownership mentality and hard work, she climbed her way to success. She taught my dad and uncles to all utilize the same mindset. And now my dad was trying to teach it to me!

***

WHEN I FIRST ARRIVED in Texas, my mother introduced me to one of her neighbors named Tamara. She was about ten or fifteen years older than I was. Her nationality was Jamaican, Asian, and Black, so she was very beautiful and difficult to ignore. Her ten-year-old daughter went to school with my younger sister, and she and my mother were friendly.

It's true that we meet some of the best people under the strangest circumstances. Soon Tamara and I forged a relationship, and over the years, Tee would prove to be one of my most trusted friends and confidantes.

The first thing that I learned about Tee was that she was a hustler. She ran her own business and knew her way around the credit game really well. One day, I mentioned that I was trying to get a new car, but my credit wasn't great. She told me that she could help me get a car and get my credit together.

To make a long story short, Tee introduced me to someone she knew at a new Credit Union. They were doing some kind of promotion. I qualified for a $30,000 personal loan, a high limit credit card, and they would even finance my car. (I know free money...right?) That didn't help my spending addiction at all!

I purchased a used BMW through their financing and had thirty bands in the bank! Yeah, I thought I was doing it big. I told my father the good news, thinking he would be proud of me. His reaction was the total opposite of what I expected. He was furious!

He said: "Pooh, you don't need a BMW. The maintenance and upkeep is too expensive. If you're gonna spend that kind of money on a car, it needs to be new and not somebody else's former problem."

"Well, I already got the car and I can't take it back. If I'm the one paying the notes, I should be allowed to get whatever kind of car I want," I answered, testing his patience by being a smarty pants.

My feelings were hurt by his reaction. I was trying to prove my independence and show my dad that I could achieve big things, just like he had. Nowhere in my wildest imagination could I imagine a scenario where a foreign car and thirty grand would be frowned upon. Especially when I hadn't broken the law, sold my soul, or given up any family secrets. Yet, my dream was suddenly becoming a nightmare. He was quite upset to say the least.

Then, as if he had hidden cameras set up in the Galleria mall, he asked: "How much money do you have left?"

How did he know that I had already been spending money? I wondered. It was true. I had given my mom some money, and although Tee didn't ask for anything, I hit her hand with a few bands for giving me the game. Of course, I purchased a few things for myself as well.

"About nineteen," I answered shamefully.

He said: "Lauren..." and I knew I had messed up. He never called me by my first name.

"You never borrow money from anyone unless you have a plan to use it to bring in more money. At least enough money to pay the debt." He paused to gather his thoughts and then added, "That little bit of money will be gone before you know it, and then you will still have the debt. How much is the interest rate?"

I was ashamed that I didn't know the answer to that important question. Can you imagine not even knowing how much you owe for the money you borrowed? I don't have to tell you how bad he tore into me about that! This man is a stomp-down hustler. He wasn't raising us to get hustled and here, because of my ignorance, I'd become the mark.

At the time when I was signing for the loans, it didn't seem to matter. All I knew was that my car note was $565 a month (cheaper than a rental car), my mom put me on her insurance, I was riding good, and I didn't have to start paying the money back until sometime next year.

I didn't dare tell him about the $15,000 credit card that was on its way in the mail. Maybe I had sold my soul. After all…I had failed miserably at the first big score I did on my own. I got the cash, but the harsh lessons I would learn about handling money would be invaluable...and painful.

***

OUR SUCCESS AND FAILURE rates are determined by many factors: the learning curve, trial and error, experience, and education. In the years to follow, I would learn many invaluable lessons that I want to share in the hope it may help some young lady or man understand the importance of making good financial moves.

My late teens and early twenties were the most significant learning period in my life.

***

HUSTLING 101: WHEN YOU'RE hustling, you need to adopt a meager living budget. The ratio of money coming in, to the amount of money going out, should be significant. The ideal ratio is 5 to 1 (or spending 20% of your earnings).

Very few people can master this technique, because we don't earn enough to use only 20% of our income and still survive. That is why we don't have what is considered "money." The vast majority of Americans are living paycheck to paycheck by design. (Ask yourself why they called the wealthy ruling class the "One Percent"? It's because 1% of the population controls 85% of the nation's wealth. That means that 99% of the country divides the remaining 15%. Google it!) Living hustle to hustle is the same thing if it doesn't provide a consistently significant source of income, comparable to your living expenses.

Realistically, the average person spends between 110 to 130% of their income. This means that most of us are spending money that we don't have. Any time you use a credit card for anything other than a strategic purchase (credit-boosting purchases that you can afford, but utilize the payment to enhance your credit score) you're spending beyond your means. In simple math, you're adding 12%

interest (or more) to each purchase for the "privilege" of paying the tab later.

This was a bad habit I picked up in college. When there's no one to give you financial guidance (or your ego won't allow you to listen), you tend to develop bad spending and saving habits. My father tried to give me the game, but I was too far gone. I had gotten a taste of the credit game and I was strung out!

***

THAT BRINGS ME TO the expensive lessons that I'm about to pass along to you for free (minus the cost of this book).

1. Never borrow money without knowing the interest rate.

2. Never borrow money without a plan for usage that will net you a profit.

3. Don't buy a used car and pay huge notes. You might as well buy something new that has a warranty and will be more dependable.

4. When you're hustling, a car is for transportation from point A to point B. If you want to flex from time to time, rent a luxury vehicle for a few days.

5. My Achilles heel at the time: Never spend money that you don't have! Credit cards are for strategic purchases only...and you must know the credit card rules. (Spending more than 30% of your card limit will lower your credit score, or FICO, up to 25 points.)

Here are a few more maxims that I've learned over the years that have helped me navigate the dangerous financial landscape. Sometimes an unconventional approach to business or money management is what sets you apart from the competition, or just allows you to hone in on your approach to meeting your financial goals. These rules apply to corporate business moguls or the common around-the-way hustler. Pay attention!

6. Fast nickels always beat slow dimes. (You would rather sell 50 bottles of water daily at 15% profit, than 10 bottles a day at 50% profit.)

7. A penny saved is a penny earned. (Never be ashamed to shop for a bargain. Walmart didn't become the world's most recognized retailer by accident. The concept of "price match" ensured any customer that they could never find the same product cheaper at any other retailer.)

8. What you make isn't as important as what you save. (The rainy day fund gets you through the storm. If you live moderately while things are relatively good financially, you can save enough to carry you through a period of financial tragedy.)

9. Scared money can't win and lost money can't spend. (In other words, invest into things that you have witnessed be successful for others. Don't be afraid to "copycat" success, like you copycat fashion or lingo. Any money spent on perishables or fads is lost and

it can never be regained...unless pawn shops start accepting used bundles of expensive hair weave!)

These are some of the hard lessons that must be learned but are not taught in most homes. Things you're definitely not going to get from a public school education. I've decided that at this point, it would be prudent of me to close this chapter with a note to parents: TEACH YOUR CHILDREN FINANCIAL RESPONSIBILITY! If you don't have good financial skills as an adult, it's probably because you weren't taught the importance of financial responsibility in your younger years. Just remember that it's never too early to start teaching your children how to save money and spend responsibly.

For more financial tips that you should teach your children see Appendix B: Financial Literacy.

Chapter Nine:
The Birth of ABC

URING MY FRESHMAN YEAR of college, I was working on a research paper dealing with suicide and mental health for a Sociology course when I came across some startling statistics about children who had committed suicide as a result of an act of bullying. I wanted to do something to help.

I was talking to my dad about it and he was like: "Pooh, we don't get bullied!" He didn't see how I would be able to relate to the victims. I wanted him to understand what I felt about the way it impacted me. I didn't necessarily have to be bullied to know the feelings of despair or helplessness firsthand. I also knew people who weren't as assertive as me and my family members.

While I don't believe that my father and uncles were bullies, I'm not naive enough to believe they weren't hyper-aggressive...to put it mildly! So, I asked myself: Why? Why did some people get bullied while others didn't?

In my mind, if we could pin down the mind state and characteristics of those who didn't accept being bullied, we'd have something. First, we needed to study bullies and victims to find out how each thought and what caused them to develop distinctive characteristics. We would then bundle that research into lessons that could alter those behaviors.

I was envisioning a scientific/social endeavor that if successful, would enable us to change the climate of our learning institutions. The funny thing was that I had no idea of the degree of difficulty that was typically involved in such a monumental task. In certain circles they call the people who attempt such a thing...doctors! All I knew was that I couldn't ignore the issue, now that I had been awakened to the reality. In an attempt to validate the process, I figured I could use my best resource as subjects for my study...my family! The problem was I had no idea where to start.

My dad told me that the first thing I needed to do was to narrow down my topic and get my research paper done. Graduate first, and then save the world!

In the weeks to follow, with his help, I got an "A" on my research paper. Further validation that I had powerful insight into the problem. The research sparked a serious interest in me, but I put those interests on the back burner for the time being and tried to focus on the immediate task at hand: school.

During that time, my dad was also in school, working on his bachelor's degree in business. He was on an accelerated pace, taking six and seven classes a semester. He earned his degree in eighteen months and graduated Magna Cum Laude with a 3.69 GPA. He said he could have finished sooner, but when Granny Deb passed away he took a couple months off from school.

Leave it to him to set a bar that none of us could compete against. Weren't we supposed to be able to surpass the levels that our parents reached in life? That was seeming all but impossible with this man in prison, but still outperforming us financially and educationally. I've learned over the years that he doesn't do it maliciously. He's just doing him and being who he is! In everything he does, his attitude is: "Go big or go home. Lead or get out of the way!" Sometimes that poses a problem for those of us who have to follow his act. I want to be the leader at some point. He was making that very difficult for his eldest child, and I needed him to get out of my light, so I could shine.

As God would have it, not long after he graduated, he was asked to participate in a mentoring program for the troubled youth at the prison he was in. The administrators were charged with the duty of housing 420 youth offenders in a secluded section of the prison. Most of the young men were gang-affiliated, violent offenders, and serving long or life sentences for every kind of crime imaginable. The transition at the prison was complete chaos. My dad said that every five minutes they were shutting the prison down for a gang fight or stabbing. The young guys were raising hell, and clearly the administration wasn't prepared for that. They didn't know what to do, so the Deputy Warden—an administrator who interacts more closely with corrections officers (COs) and prisoners than the Warden—suggested they enlist some of the older inmates for suggestions to help.

Keep in mind that juveniles fall into a special class when it comes to crime and punishment. They can't be treated like adults or disciplined with the same methods. Apparently, these young guys knew it too. They understood that no matter what they did, they couldn't be put into long-term solitary confinement or be housed on the adult side of the prison. They definitely took advantage of that.

The Warden needed an effective program and fast. These young prisoners were completely out of control.

My father told me that he didn't have time for prison politics. He was about to start a Master's degree program, and what the administrators were asking for required a lot. I said: "Dad, this could be good for you. Give it a try. You owe that much to society." My statement gave him a nudge, but he was still reluctant. I added: "We (meaning he would be doing all the work) could create a program and beta test it on these kids. If it works, then we can implement it in the schools out here." I can always tell when I say something worthy of my father's undivided attention. He gets quiet and then asks me: "How would I do it?" That was the pivotal moment when I knew that he would be my main source of assistance for whatever I decided to do in regard to preventing youth suicides because of bullying.

***

WE SPENT THE NEXT couple of weeks working on the logistics of the program. It was originally called "Real Talk." (Really original, right?) Eventually my dad and the young prisoners would come up with the name "Anti-Bully Crusaders"—ABC.

My dad submitted a proposal, and one week later he was given a platform. It started with three separate groups of fifteen to twenty Black, White, and Latino prisoners between the ages of sixteen and twenty-one. He hand-picked his facilitators (prisoner program representatives), and to the amazement of the administrators, they convinced the young prisoners to come together for a thirty-day peace, acceptance, and tolerance treaty. Understand that this was over 400 testosterone-fueled, convicted felons, all under the age of twenty-two! The project was so effective in the first month of its implementation that critical incidents at the prison went from 480 per month to under 150. It was unbelievable.

I asked my dad how he was able to convince a wild bunch like that to cooperate with him, when the prison administration couldn't. He said: "Well, two things. I was once a troubled youth myself. What I do know is that young people really want to learn, and for the most part, they really want to be good people too. Sometimes circumstances and environments won't allow them to be. Especially when they haven't been given the necessary tools to navigate the pitfalls. That's a whole other conversation for another time. And two: You have to be relatable. If you want to reach and teach the youth, you have to be of the youth. You've got to speak their language. Not only do they have to know you care, but they have to know that you have truly been where they are, mentally and physically. And trust me, they can sniff out a fake a mile away. So never lie to them."

Going forward, I knew this methodology would be the core of our future programming. I made a mental note that young people will listen to and do almost anything you want, as long as you love, teach, and be loyal, and you don't mistreat them.

Truth be told, we really didn't know what was happening at the time, but we knew we were onto something big. The head officials and administrators wanted to know how our program was able to accomplish this miracle. We took full advantage of the occasion to slide in some other incentive-based programs, just to see if they would work as well.

We began to invite influential men and women, as well as leaders, from other communities. We also invited the administrative personnel and other influential inmates on the compound to open seminars for discussions, suggestions, and to participate in our movement for "Peace." I was able to personally collaborate with the programs coordinator and invite some of our celebrity friends and family members to visit the prison and speak to the youth. Amazingly, we even convinced a billionaire co-founder of Bizdom University's incubator-accelerator program to come in. Of course, this gave us a certain amount of leverage because we had proven ourselves out the gate.

As a bonus, my dad actually convinced the warden to host a banquet for our assembly. This was a practice that hadn't been approved inside the prison in years. They all agreed that if my father and his fellow prisoners could change the atmosphere of the prison, they deserved a banquet. That's actually how we came up with the concept of a graduation ceremony as an incentive for the kids who completed the program in the schools. The rest is history.

The ABC project was born out of this effort. What organization can say that their program was beta-tested in a prison setting, among the people society considers the worst of the worst?

The Michigan Department of Corrections will never give my father or his fellow inmates the credit they deserve for ABC changing the climate of that prison and helping to bring out the best in those young men. Of course, they took the credit. Every warden, deputy, and facility member involved got a promotion on the backs of my dad and his partners' free labor. Hell, they need to be thanking me for convincing my dad to participate in their program. I ain't holding my breath, but aside from the obvious, I learned that receiving credit is secondary to actual success.

What happened from that simple challenge changed my dad's life, my life, and the lives of all those young men, forever. The prison gave us the opportunity to experiment and eventually perfect our life's mission. They got a sample, but we own the blueprint. As someone in my circle is fond of saying: "Why take credit when you can take cash?"

***

THE ANTI-BULLY CRUSADERS organization had become my primary focus. My father and I had become obsessively preoccupied with creating our own program that would impact the youth in learning centers and the community in general. We learned that if it could happen inside a prison, it could happen anywhere.

While revising the program and creating a curriculum, we knew we had to maintain the integrity of the original program and simultaneously make sure it would be relevant to the needs of children and teens everywhere.

While I had a ton of suggestive input, the real work was done by my dad. He was responsible for writing the ABC Workbook and Facilitator's Manual, and I was responsible for all the legwork out here. It was a fair division of labor.

Can you imagine the degree of dedication and intelligence that it took to accomplish this feat? This man essentially wrote a college level textbook, singlehandedly. That required that he basically teach himself psychology and applied behavioral science; study and reevaluate the social engineering of current anti-bullying programs; and become an author in less than two years—something usually accomplished by a group of scholars. The idea that this man even considered this to be a reasonable request, simply because his daughter asked him to, is mind-blowing to me!

It took about a year and a half, but it was well worth all the critiques and laborious efforts. Everyone to whom I gave a sneak peek was impressed and couldn't believe my dad and I had come up with such an innovative program. Not to blow my own horn, but there was a consensus that the ABC curriculum was unmatched even by the scholars in this field.

ABC was no longer just a thought. It was coming into fruition, and the haters were out there on the dancefloor.

Most people knew my father's level of education and intelligence, so they didn't question the integrity of the program or creative process. It was more like they were jealous that they hadn't come up with the idea first or managed to maintain a relationship like what my father and I had. I guess that part was understandable. I just would have imagined there would be more positive reinforcement; but I've heard that: "Nothing sucks like success."

81

While the haters didn't mind taking shots at me, they were careful about insulting my father. Close associates knew that the consequence of offending me would be a direct assault on my dad as well, so most were just disingenuously cordial. It's a shame how some of your own family members will try to sabotage your opportunities to become successful. It showed me the truth of why my father always said: "Friends and family will drag you through the mud. You gotta love 'em but you ain't gotta do business with 'em."

As a rule of thumb, we generally don't do business with family members who are not business oriented, or don't have any business experience. That's a disaster waiting to happen. Instead, we give to them, with no expectations of anything in return. After all, they're family, and we have a moral obligation to them whether we like them or not! And don't get it twisted; you don't have to like someone to love them.

Again, I would soon have to learn these cold lessons the hard way.

Chapter Ten:
Envy vs Jealousy

F OR THE LIFE OF me, I'll never be able to understand why people hate on each other. If someone is more fortunate, smarter, luckier, or doing better in general, we should be happy for them. They are an example of the possibilities for self-improvement. This should be especially true if the person is our kinfolk.

While the words "envy" and "jealousy" are often used synonymously, I've been taught that they have two very distinctive meanings. Envy often denotes a form of admiration. It's like seeing someone with a unique skill and saying: "Damn she's good. I wish I could do that." Or when a good friend says they "envy your marriage." It's a positive affirmation of your good fortune being recognized. When a person envies the fact that they don't have a skill set, it has nothing to do with having ill will towards the person who possesses the skill. It's more about them and their desires.

On the other hand, jealousy is when you see someone with something and wish that they didn't have it. For example, you'll hear someone say: "I work seven days a week and I don't drive a BMW. She don't even have a job and got one?" OR..."How she get man like that? She don't look better than me." This person speaks as if the other doesn't deserve it. We call that: HATING on a playa! When someone displays feeling of dissatisfaction because you're doing well, or praying on your downfall, you have to be careful. They have actually announced their intention to sabotage any further success, if given the opportunity.

We also have to learn to spot this poisonous attribute in our supposed "friends" who don't display it towards us, per se. They soon will. As my uncle likes to say: "If a snake didn't use its teeth to bite, it would just be called a worm. Don't be no fool!"

My father once told me that jealousy is the worst of all hates because you never know exactly why a person hates you. It could be your car, your hair, your man, or something as trivial as your beautiful smile. It could be anything. If you or I have offended one another, then we know where we stand. But if I haven't done anything to you and you hate me, there is something psychotic and deranged about that. That's dangerous! You may need to seek some professional counseling for that problem. My advice is to spend less time worrying about someone else's life and more time on bossing yours up!

My dad also has a philosophy about the difference in how men and women approach conflict or perceived threats. It all boils down to ego, desire, and discipline. Usually when a man is defending his manhood, he acts out as a way to not be seen as weak or a chump. That's one reason why so many young black men are killing each other (ego!). Something happens to offend the perceived level of respect, and he loses his cool, goes mad, insane, crazy! Absent discipline, he reacts to whims and a desire to prove a point. He does some of the stupidest shit. All for what? Immediate gratification for the desired effect.

Women, on the other hand, are more vindictive and conniving. Sneaky, even. (His words, not mine!) Because they are typically less physical than men, women have perfected the art of lying in wait for the perfect opportunity to strike. They can disguise hatred for long periods of time. Women are the masters of deception. Throughout history, they have turned men against each other and started wars! Now that's power!

Women who have mastered these skills are dangerous and often our "friends." Have you ever paid attention to nature? Female animals are the most vicious of every species, from the smallest to the largest. The female black widow spider mates and then kills the male. The female lion does the hunting for food. Need I say more? What makes you think the human female is any different?

These are the analogies my dad always uses to help me see the deeper meaning of what he is teaching. Thus, he has warned me that my most dangerous enemy is the one who is jealous of me and close enough to strike without warning. One who has the ability to camouflage herself and disguise her hatred for long periods of time. A snake that blends into the landscape so well that you have to look really closely to spot her, but once spotted, you should never ignore the danger.

Men are not as much of a threat in terms of jealousy, because we are suspicious of them from the start and therefore not apt to miss the clues. In fact, even a man who hates you probably only does so because you don't love him. Offer him your friendship and watch how his energy shifts. Words to live by.

***

MY FATHER FINALLY FINISHED the ABC Workbook and Facilitator's Manual (by himself!). We found an editor in Sarasota, Florida, and she found the illustrator. She was so impressed by our work that she edited the workbook for free.

"I love your cause. This is my contribution, free of charge. Good luck. ~ Carol."

That was a great gesture and a beautiful way to start a working relationship. We were grateful, but we still needed to have both the ABC Workbook and the Facilitator's Manual typeset, page layout designed, and illustrations added. We needed her! Her quote was more expensive than her overseas counterparts listed on Fiverr.com and Upwork.com, but there were no language or time barriers. We were able to work with her in real time, during normal business hours, set up phone conferences, and get good industry advice. She was good at what she does and worth her weight in gold.

Our first edition was complete, and it was time to test our product before bringing it to market. A friend of mine, a teacher in the Uplift School District in Fort Worth, allowed us to speak to several of her classes. While my father was proud of me for coming up with a game plan and seeing it through, he assured me that I would need to find people who were good public speakers and knew their way around a stage for our public seminars. This went for the classroom and teaching the curriculum as well. He insisted that we use "professional people."

In my mind, I had this. Instead of doing all that, I assembled a team of friends and family members, and we hosted a couple of small seminars and workshops. None of us had actual experience in speaking or teaching, but we didn't do too badly.

That was the worst thing that could have happened to me. It supported the wrong business model (mediocrity over excellence). I thought I was onto something. My girls and I could get this done ourselves. To quote my dad's infamous words: "Too easy, right?"

Once again, I underestimated his business acumen and experience. And once again, I would be learning the hard lessons for myself.

Chapter Eleven:
"People Grow Apart"

AY AND I HAD been the first ones to move into my mother's house and the first to move out. I needed my own space for a number of reasons. Even though I didn't have a job and hadn't yet gotten good with handling money, Jay was. This was our first apartment together, an accomplishment that made me happy, excited, and proud because the place was really nice. I was seemingly following in the footsteps of my parents, by doing adult things with my man.

Jay had a swagger about him and he liked nice things. I have to give him credit, because he always did his best by me. Personally, he'd settled into a comfort zone. To him, life was good. I get it...you have a nice job, making more money than you've ever made, have newfound credit, a new car, an apartment, and are playing house with your first love. What wasn't to love about that situation for a young twenty-something?

The reality was that I wasn't afforded the same luxuries. I didn't have any of those things of my own, and playing house wasn't good enough for me. At that particular moment, I felt compelled to take drastic action because there were things I wanted, and I had to figure out what to do to accomplish those things. Going to school and being taken care of may have been enough for some girls, but it wasn't enough for LeRoy Washington's daughter! I've always had an insatiable hunger for more living inside of me and pushing me to be greater that I currently am. I had to figure out my own life!

Truth be told, I believe that the sudden awakening of that energy was the beginning of Jay's and my real problems. I started believing in myself. I didn't want to be a dependent woman, just being taken care of. Of course, I wanted my man to do nice things for me, but I also wanted to do the same things for myself and my family without restrictions or permission!

Nowadays, I can see how this might have come across as ungrateful or confusing to Jay. He was just doing what he believed was the proper thing for a man to do. I know that he had honorable intentions because we had essentially grown up together. Many of his firsts were mine as well. That was the gift and the curse of exploring adulthood with someone who had no advantage on the learning curve. The closest of friends would soon become live-in adversaries. The revelation that we wanted different things out of life shocked us both, and we struggled to define a relationship where we were equals.

I'm not the type of person anyone can hold back from getting my own. I needed my own money, a career that satisfied my desire for freedom, and the ability to create lanes for others. Clearly, that wasn't going to happen at GM!

Jay and I attempted to navigate the issues that arose, but as time flew by, the distance between us seemed to expand. Over the years I guess it had become painfully obvious that we had different goals, and the journey to fulfillment was pulling us apart. Our relationship had become toxic, and we were breaking up, only to make up, again and again. I was unhappy in the relationship, and when you're not happy, it's difficult to make someone else happy. It was time for a change!

I'm no relationship guru, but I once read that: "There's nothing worse than staying in a relationship for too long; but even worse is when you know you didn't do enough to save it." At the time I couldn't tell if I had stayed too long or hadn't done enough to make it work. The bad thing about breakups is that you never know how the other person is affected. Honestly, I was too embarrassed to ask my parents for advice on my failed relationship. That meant that we'd have to figure this one out on our own.

Chapter Twelve:
Summer Sixteen

"I got a really big team; they need some really big rings
Some really big things.... What a time to be alive..."

Drake & Future, "Big Things

I T WAS SUMMER 2016. I was in Texas, living with Jay, still going to school. I had made some new friends while exploring some business opportunities. While I appeared to be doing well in the eyes of others, I wasn't happy with my personal life or accomplishments. I wanted more and knew I had the potential and means to get it! I just hadn't figured it out yet. I was determined to find my niche, and with my dad on my team, I knew it was only a matter of time.

My original crew all made plans to get back together for a home visit in Georgia. It was perfect timing, because I needed some time away to get my head together and figure some things out. Plus, it would be good to see the girls.

Our lives had all taken different paths since we were in high school. Coincidentally, none of us had babies or were married yet. My girl, Neha, was a second-generation Palestinian Muslim, born in America. Neha had the exotic look of a Palestinian Rosario Dawson. She was just beautiful, with thick wavy hair and that certain flair that said: "Boss Chick." You can imagine what kind of drive had been instilled in her to achieve in America.

Her father was a big time real estate broker who was never home. Her childhood house actually had a real elevator. It looked more like a hotel or resort than a mansion. We'd had a lot of fun when we spent time over there as kids. Neha had an all-expenses-paid, full ride college experience and made good by graduating from the University of Miami. I was proud of her. At the time she was the only one of us to graduate from college on time. She was currently interning at a record label and living her dream. Despite these factors, she didn't seem happy with her life, either.

My friend Paris, on the other hand, had it rougher than any of us coming up. She came from a large family of Black American Muslims and humble beginnings. At the time, she was working and going to school in ATL. Paris was a pretty girl, with a soft cinnamon complexion and classic features. Oval face, full lips, great cheekbones, and slightly slanted eyes that were the color of Lipton Iced Tea. She always wore her hair long and her fashion was lit.

What I loved about Paris is that even though she didn't have much, she never complained. I think it made us closer than the other girls because she understood my plight as well. She always seemed to be the happiest of us all. Apparently "adversity builds character," as my father would say. Over the years, she and I have remained friends through it all.

Then there were Mahogany and Katie. Mahogany was still living in Atlanta also, working and putting herself through school.

Katie was the White girl of the bunch. What I loved about her is that she never tried to act outside of her culture. It was cool to be different, and she didn't fake the funk to fit in. She was what we deemed the "all-American privileged White girl," but she was genuine, and that was all that mattered to us. She was settled in New York, living out her dream of working for some big-time brokerage firm. It was the first time I had seen both of them since graduation.

Now, my girl GG came through on baller status! Everything about the way she presented herself said that she was a boss. It wasn't difficult to tell someone who really had it going on from those who just looked the part, once you knew what to look for. GG was the girl who I would call my California Barbie. She had a smooth cocoa complexion, with a heart-shaped face, D cups, round ass, and the swagger of a Hollywood actress. She easily owned a room when she entered.

Being that she was a Cali girl, GG wasn't impressed by the Atlanta culture and didn't stay long. She was originally from LA, and when her father had gotten locked up (something we had in common) she moved to Atlanta with relatives. As soon as she finished school, she went back home. I don't know what she was doing out in Cali, but she was papered up. (Well, I guess I do, but my dad said that we don't get to tell other people's secrets or stories without their permission. Keep it cute, but keep it gangsta!) So I'll just say this: she was the real go-get-it-out-the-mud hustler of the crew. A self-made woman! She had bread and she had a plan. I respect how everybody gets their paper.

I asked Jazmine (Jazz) to join us. Jazz was my homegirl from waaaay back in the day when I still lived in Flint, Michigan. I'm talking pre-k, first, and second grade—which now felt like a whole other lifetime. She was the only friend I really had from that era in my life who managed to stay in touch over the years. That gave us a special bond, like immigrants who move to a foreign country. We knew where it all began.

If Zoey Kravitz had a twin sister separated at birth, it was Jazz. Not only did she look like her, she displayed the same free spirit and was more at ease in jeans and sneakers than high heels and skirts. She had a cool vibe and was the only one of us who didn't grow up in ATL. I had introduced her to all the girls, and she fit in perfectly. Real people tend to have the ability.

To my surprise, even Ley was there. She was in the Army, stationed in Korea, at home on leave. Of all the places and things? I never saw Ley as the type to go into the military. She was very beautiful and could have easily became a model—light skinned, with an athletic body, runner's legs, and a face that put you in the mind of a movie actress at first glance. A more sultry version of Essence Atkins.

People say she looked like my mother when my mom was in high school. They did bear a striking resemblance. That was part of the reason people who had just met us used to think we were biological sisters.

It was like having our own class reunion. We had all grown up, and time had flown by so fast. This was the first time since high school that we were all able to get together. While I had seen some of the girls off and on, I hadn't seen Ley in six years. Everyone knew what had happened between us. We'd been super tight back then, so our falling out was like Destiny's Child breaking up. I didn't want to make it awkward, so I was cordial. To be honest, I was never really mad at Ley, and I was happy to see her. It was her mother and sister who I felt were wrong. I guess she had to side with her family.

Now, though, we were all grown women enjoying the opportunity to reunite. That alone overrode any petty emotions that may have lingered. However, after the usual catching up and exchanging a few niceties, combined with a few drinks, to my amazement, Ley apologized to me in front of everyone. She even agreed that her mother was tripping.

We all had a good laugh about the whole ordeal. After all, we had nearly come to blows over me standing up for myself. I hadn't stolen her boyfriend and she hadn't crashed my car. It wasn't even our beef. It was funny how what could make you cry, could also make you laugh.

Both of us had grown so far past the moment that it was as if it never happened. Plus, the long overdue, sincere apology put the icing on the cake. Bygones were just that—a thing of the past that inadvertently made me stronger.

I was actually proud of Ley. It was really brave of her to go to the Army. That was something that none of the rest of us could ever do. She was certainly braver than we were.

The conversations about lifestyles were to be expected, but my life paled in comparison with the rest of the ladies. They were all traveling, working their dream jobs, and in what appeared to be healthy relationships. I don't know if everyone was fronting or keeping it a buck, so I just remained quiet and didn't speak much about the things I had going on. What was apparent was that we were all in our early twenties, attractive, and hungry.

I was happy when Neha's phone rang, and she motioned for everyone to be quiet while she put the phone on speaker.

"M, I got you on speaker. I'm here with my girls. Can you comp us for the backstage passes?" she asked in a casual voice that spoke of expectation.

"I told you I got y'all. We still on for that one thing, right?" he asked with a flirty tone.

"Boy, don't play! You know you ain't getting no pussy, so don't be acting all mannish in front of my girls. But a deal is a deal. I will introduce you to Timbaland and Missy, like I said I would." She made a face at us that said: "the nerve of men."

"I didn't mean it like that," he shot back, laughing. "Don't be so mean, Sis. You know I got you. How many tickets y'all need, and what hotel are y'all at? I'll be there in thirty minutes."

Neha gave us the thumbs up. She and Paris both knew Future's deejay/producer, Metro Booming, personally. They said that we went to school with him and tried to help me remember who he was, but I couldn't recall. I hate when someone remembers me and I don't remember them. It's almost dismissive and disrespectful. I gotta get better with that.

Future was headlining at the Fox, and it was sure to be the event of the night. Metro never made it to our hotel room, but he sent over the backstage passes, VIP passes for the after-party, and a party bus to accommodate us for the night. All of this, along with an apology note that read: "Sorry, ladies, I got caught up with sound check and other last minute show business. I look forward to meeting you all tonight. Be safe, have fun, and everything is on me!"

"Ladies, this is how we do it in the industry," Neha bragged. "Nothing but the best for my BF's for life!"

It was a long night of partying and socializing. I hadn't done that in years and had almost forgotten what it felt like to have fun. The following morning, the ladies met at the hotel restaurant for breakfast. I wasn't due to leave Atlanta for a few more days, but some of the ladies had to fly out that afternoon. Neha was leaving the same day as I was and wanted Paris, Ley, and me to stay the remainder of the days with her at her parents' house. We quickly agreed. It wasn't hard to convince us! The four of us were actually the core of our ensemble, so it was pretty poetic that it happened that way. There are those times in life when you just feel like there is a divine force in control, guiding you to great things. This was one of those moments.

There you had it. Just like that, the party was moved to the Big House we had all admired as children. We decided to stay in that night, eat some good food, and just catch up. Neha, prying like she does, said: "Lauren, I don't remember you saying much about your life yesterday. Is everything all right with you?"

You picked up on that? I thought to myself. It became apparent that there was no escaping it this time. While my life seemed to be the least interesting of the group, I didn't want them to think I wasn't happy or come across as a Debbie Downer. That meant that I had to have a quick comeback.

To lower the expectations, I said: "Well, my life isn't as exciting as all of yours. I've just been working on starting a nonprofit with my father."

I was stunned when they all seemed to be interested. I couldn't tell if they were genuinely intrigued, if it was a noble gesture, or just an act to see what my dad and I had going on. I get that sometimes from people. I didn't understand it back in the day, but I do now.

People who view you as competition or may envy you will act as if they are interested in your life, when they are really spying to learn what your advantage may be. That's why my dad repeatedly told me to keep things close to the vest when I started handling his affairs. It was never wise to share your plans with people who don't play a part in bringing them to life.

However, I knew that even if they didn't want me to outshine them, no one in the room wanted to see me fail. I pulled up the ABC Workbook and Instructors Manual on my phone. My dad had done an exceptional job with the curriculum. I did the layout, and we shared the title of coauthor. I didn't realize that being a published author was such a big thing, but the girls made a big deal out of it. I do have to admit that the project was well put together and very professional.

Each lady offered to help and actually came up with some amazing ideas as we discussed the problem with suicide and bullying among the youth. We could all relate to similar feelings at times in life.

Right on cue, as if he knew I needed his help, the phone rang "This is a collect call from: Saalih, an innate at a Michigan Correctional Facility. To accept the charges, press one." I accepted the call.

"Hey, Dad," I said excitedly.

"Hey, beautiful," he answered with our usual greeting.

"I'm here with the girls in the ATL," I announced, with the phone on speaker.

"Hey, Dad!" they all said in unison.

They had been doing that since we were kids. It made me feel good that none of my friends looked down on me or on my dad for being incarcerated. In fact, they had a great deal of reverence for him and respected our relationship. Each girl in my crew had told me on separate occasions that they wished their fathers were more like mine, or that they had the kind of relationship we have. Everyone knew that my dad was my best friend and confidant! Over the years, they all jumped on his Jpay (the prison email system) and developed their own personal relationships with him in which they could get fatherly advice and guidance.

"I was telling the girls about the Anti-Bully Crusaders and some of our plans. They came up with some pretty good ideas too!" I informed him.

Immediately Neha chimed in, excitedly talking about possibilities and the necessity of such a program. Paris followed up with her perspective on why ABC was a groundbreaking idea. My dad listened and then eloquently spoke about the subject with a form of knowledge and professionalism that I knew I'd have to master someday.

Here we were, young, college-educated women with degrees, being educated by a man that society had thrown away for a minimum of forty-two years. My father's voice had a mesmerizing effect. He knew his stuff and he somehow always found a way to include everyone in the conversation. It was something that I couldn't explain, but he had it in spades. He also had the unique talent of allowing you to present an idea that he had previously thought of, but made you feel he was grateful that you had presented it to him. It proved to be an effective tactic in promoting confidence-building. It encouraged people to express their views without insecurities. You would be surprised at how often that yields an ingenious perspective.

Our conversation and exchange of ideas went on for several fifteen-minute calls. Needless to say, when he got finished hosting our think tank, everyone was pumped to bring ABC to life! Even after he said goodbye, that was all we talked about for the rest of the night.

At one point, Ley said: "Lauren, I'm serious about ABC being a great humanitarian act, and I would love to be a part of it. If you and your dad will have me on board, I'll even move to Dallas when I discharge next month."

That was a huge statement and boost for my confidence. Even if it was just words. With the way I was feeling about being stuck in the mud while my girls thrived, any positive feedback felt wonderful. I didn't think that Ley was serious at the time, but I was thinking, *Man, it would be fun to have one of the girls down here permanently, to help navigate the storms of young adulthood.* I was at the stage in my life where I could use some encouragement. I felt totally stagnated in my relationship with Jay, but hadn't found the reason to take a leap into the unknown as of yet. I knew that with someone from my team around, the energy shift would prove to be dynamic, as well as force me to represent. We didn't have slouches in our circle. So I spoke for me and my dad and invited Ley to come.

Days later, I left the reunion with my girls feeling like everyone's life was so much more exciting than mine. I felt like I was stuck in a vacuum, constantly being sucked into a life that I didn't want. My daily routine was on repeat cycle, like a hamster on a wheel, and it was beginning to evoke feelings of desperation. I remember being on the plane ride home, thinking: *Damn, I gotta get my life together. And quick!*

I spent some time reading over notes I had taken from the girls and I had the ABC Facilitators Manual pulled up on my laptop. I'd been given a first-class upgrade and was sitting next to an older White woman. I recall thinking that her perfume smelled classy and expensive. I paid attention to her clothes, shoes, and even her French manicure that indicated money! I could tell that she was important. She had obviously been paying attention to me as well.

After a while, she said, "Excuse me, if you don't mind me asking, what is that anti- bullying stuff you're reading?"

That started a conversation about ABC and how my father and I had created the concept. I informed her that while in school, I had come across the national statistics for suicide among children and how bullying played a major part. I explained how I'd been so deeply moved by the information that I spoke to my dad about it, and he had an idea. At the time, my father worked as a youth facilitator in the prison where he was in Michigan. His job was to help provide solutions for youth offenders in the HYTA (Home Youth Trainees Act) Program. The goal was to assist in finding ways to avoid returning to prison through self-esteem and critical thinking training. The program selected adult role models that the younger guys would respect. Because of my dad's accomplishments and influence inside the walls, he was a shoo-in.

Come to find out, the woman next to me was a Board of Education Trustee in the state of Texas, where I lived. We talked... Well, she talked, and I listened for the entire flight home. In the end, she offered to help us get a Class One Certification (very important) when I got things in order. I couldn't believe that such a huge connection had fallen into my lap. We exchanged information and vowed to keep in touch. I could immediately tell that she wasn't just talking. She believed in what we were doing. While I'd enjoyed the company of my friends for that week, meeting this woman felt like that divine guidance I was speaking about. It made the trip worthwhile and validated that we were onto something big. You never know when or where you will meet someone who can change your life forever!

***

SHORTLY AFTER I GOT home, Jay and I mutually decided that we both needed a break. Neither of us was happy with how things were, nor did we have a plan on how to move forward. We agreed that when our lease was up, we would go our separate ways. Looking back, I was so indecisive during that period in my life. Jay and I had been in a relationship, on and off, for our entire teens and young adult lives. We were stuck in the comfort zone of familiarity. All I knew was him. He was my first and only love.

Despite the fact that things weren't always peachy between us, they weren't always bad either. He was never physically abusive, but it was one breakup after another, just to make up again. That routine was getting old. The daily arguments over the smallest things were becoming toxic, dysfunctional, and depressing. And as hard as it is to admit, it wasn't always his fault. I did my share of dumb things as well. I guess the week apart had given us both time to put our personal lives and goals into perspective. At this point we were just growing apart, and I didn't want things to end messy. I was actually hoping we could remain friends, respect each other, and have the type of love for one another like my parents had—for the rest of our lives!

I don't want to sound cold-hearted, but ladies, when it's time to move on; it's time to move on! When you fail to do so, you risk losing respect and integrity. You also hurt the other person in the equation when you know that you can no longer give 100% to the relationship.

Jay and I weren't married and we didn't have any children. I was in my early twenties and had a few dollars of my own. Finally, there was nothing standing in my way of being great. There were no more excuses. Now, I could live my life for me, instead of living for him! The concept of "two heads are better than one" should make relationships feel like support systems, not adversaries. It's bad when together is worse than apart.

I shared my situation with my father. He always had a practical way of putting things into perspective and said: "Well, Pooh, things happen. The most important thing is that both of you are okay and have mutually decided to move forward with your lives without anybody getting physically or emotionally hurt."

He then added, "Your mother and I are better friends now than we ever were as lovers. With your lover, you have expectations and needs that MUST be met! With a friend, you accept them with their flaws and for who they are. Not who you want them to be. That's the problem; couples forget how to remain friends once they become lovers."

Trust me, that's valuable advice for young couples out there who are struggling with the friendship inside of your relationship. The key word is "couple" (two heads, right?). When I would complain to my dad about my man's lack of ambition, he would remind me that "Barack Obama wasn't the president when he and Michelle first met." In that moment, I realized that my father and Jay had a man-to-man bond and personal relationship that had nothing to do with me! Even though we weren't married, I think that my dad liked the idea of me having someone in my life to watch over me and to take care of me. But I also know that he doesn't respect mediocrity and was hoping that Jay and I could accomplish what he and Mom failed to achieve in both love and success!

In my naivety, I failed to realize that my dad was once a young Black man trying to find his way. He understood Jay's dilemma better than I ever could from the perspective of a young woman.

Nowadays, I can appreciate that, but times are changing, and with all due respect: Men, why does every man want a Michelle Obama, but yet you don't expect yourself to be presidential? Like Barack Obama presidential? Doesn't it stand to reason that in order to attract a particular type of energy, you have to exhibit the same?

Question: Is he more of a man simply because of his job title? Did his wife have more potential than the woman you envision as your future First Lady? If so, maybe you should shop in a less expensive store. In my world, it takes iron to sharpen iron, and the price of gold is still measured by the ounce. Like Lil' Wayne said: "Today I went shopping and talk is still cheap." Men, sometimes we ambitious women just need you to be the machine behind our success as well. Think about that!

Don't get me wrong, President Barack Obama and First Lady Michelle were iconic. They were special in the way that they represented a magical example of class, culture, success, and Black love! I'm not minimizing their accomplishments. However, I'm suggesting that they should not be the last to do it. They raised the bar in terms of possibilities and really represented us well. He was definitely the best president of my lifetime. Aside from the obvious, what I really admire most about Barack was how he gave Michelle the credit she deserved, highlighting the role she played in the making of his success, as well as keeping him grounded. In his book, he says that after winning the election, they were celebrating his historic victory when Michelle looked over at him and whispered that he may have won the presidency, but he was still taking the girls to school in the morning. I thought that was such a powerful moment for Black women.

To many Americans, the Obamas are the epitome of real Black love and success. In each of their biographies, they speak about their individual journey and how relationships require a great deal of respect, love, and patience. However, in my personal observation, their common denominator is understanding that having a strong friendship is the key to having a great relationship. Again, "The problem with most relationships is that people forget how to be friends."

***

I PICKED UP LEY from the DFW airport. Since the reunion in Georgia weeks before, we had talked on the phone daily about apartment shopping, healthy living, exercising, and getting back on our A-game. Coincidentally, she had just gotten out of a long-term relationship as well. She'd gone through a depression phase and was on the rebound.

I wasn't trying to go through a mental thing about Jay. He seemed perfectly fine moving on, so I was also single and ready to mingle. Often when people break up, or fail at something, their attitude becomes "I gotta go harder to make a comeback." That was my attitude. I was all about upgrading! Ley and I quickly found a three-bedroom, three-bath apartment in a high-rise downtown. Paris decided that she would join us when her lease was up in four more months. The rent was $4,000 per month. I knew that I could cover my half. My only other real bills were my car note and insurance!

Needless to say, my father wasn't too happy about it. He thought I was getting in way over my head. He gave me the speech: "You're too busy trying to look rich, instead of getting rich! You need to be on a ramen noodle budget and stack your chips."

I wasn't going to say anything disrespectful, but hell, I didn't eat nobody's noodles, I sarcastically thought to myself. My dad had the wrong girl in mind. Surely his daughter could manage without slumming for 10¢ noodles.

Instead, I said, "Dad, I'm a young lady and I need nice things."

His response was typically pragmatic: "You don't need material things to validate your worth. Those things will come with time. You'll acquire and accumulate them while hustling."

Of course, I argued, "That's easy for you to say. You're a man who has already had all the things that most people want."

"That's why I know the pitfalls you're about to run into better than you," he advised.

I wasn't trying to hear anything that he was saying. We had plans. We were young, smart, single, and had a few dollars. I had no doubt that we were going to make it.

Foolishly, I thought that we would figure it out as we went along. It couldn't be that hard. I knew some pretty dumb people who had found a way to "get by" with less than we had. Like so many people who have been ruined by ARROGANCE, not listening to my father would soon have me learning the hard lessons of life...*again!*

Chapter Thirteen:
Missed Opportunities

A S THE OLDEST AND only girl of my father's three children, I had unique perspective within our family dynamic. First, I had a bird's-eye view of the effect an absent father had on young boys. Even more importantly, aside from my own experience, I learned the struggles of womanhood from watching my mom attempt to balance the family without my dad's presence.

My youngest brother, "Bruh," shares both my mom and dad, while DJ is my dad's second child, by an outside relationship. My father often refers to my brothers as his "ghetto twins" because they were born only a few months apart.

My brothers often saw things differently than I did, regarding their relationship with my dad. For most of my life, I assumed it was because I'd had more time with him prior to his incarceration. A two-year jumpstart can make a world of difference to a parent-child relationship. (Again, I reiterate that my father has been incarcerated since I was four years old. I say this to emphasize the effort that he obviously put forth, in order to have such a monumental impact on me, even today.)

As we got older, my perspective changed about the possible reasons I accepted my dad's guidance more than my brothers. Some of it boils down to personality type, sense of direction, personal goals, and level of understanding. While we all inherited a portion of his unique intelligence and ambition, we cultivated those talents in different ways.

My brothers Bruh and DJ both inherited their hustler's mentality from my pops. Neither of them would ever find themselves lost as to how to get some money. I find it intriguing to see their minds work when breaking down, dissecting, or analyzing ways to make a dollar. It's amazing how they process information on the fly and come up with the same ideas without even talking to one another. They are both masters at monetizing, maximizing, and capitalizing on any hustle. In my personal observation, both of my brothers seem to have a great deal of respect for my dad, but DJ seems to harbor some deep resentments as well. Most of his gripes are valid. That goes without saying. It would be difficult for any parent who has been absent for decades (for any reason) to defend themselves against the reasons behind a child's emotional distance.

Now that I'm older, I am more capable of understanding DJ's perspective. However, I try to emphasize that we're adults now, and at some point we have to grow beyond the things that affected us in our adolescence. We eventually have to find a way to reconcile our differences. You can't live in the past, haunted by the things that happened or mistakes already made.

I believe that someone who constantly looks backward can't see what's right in front of them, or ahead into the future. The truth of the matter is that even "justified" anger has a negative effect on the person who refuses to let go. If the feelings of despair or neglect consume you to the point where you can't achieve a healthy progression in life, then you have harmed yourself more than the initial injury.

It has been my burden to witness such a loving bond being scarred by things left unsaid (and unexplained). In terms of this subject, it's only right that my brother tells his side of the story himself, so I'm not going to comment any further. Nevertheless, if I could offer him some advice as it relates to our father, it would be this: Reach out to him. You know where he's at. Be straight up with him. He only respects the truth, and your father does not pity weakness. I know from experience that even if he could read your mind, he'd still make you say what you're thinking. I made some of those critical mistakes myself, in the past. Our father doesn't like a crybaby and despises those who make excuses. One of his favorite sayings is: "I don't like anything weak, not even my Koolaid." AND he drinks his coffee black. Who does that?

On the other hand, now that my brother Bruh is locked up and sober, he admires the hell out of Dad! All he talks about is Pops. I'm like; "Fool, I've been telling you this your whole life!" It's not that his prior feelings were invalid; it's just that sometimes parents are victims of circumstances that are beyond the scope of their momentary intelligence.

With one direct conversation, my brothers might understand that our dad was only a few years older than they are now when he made the decisions that altered everyone's future. If they could hear from his lips just how lost he had been in his youth, they might realize that he is only human. They may even see more of themselves in him and respect their ability to transform into powerful men. Just like him.

I understand that "Father" is a title of extreme reverence. To be duly crowned comes with great pride as well as limitless expectations. In fact, I expect that if I were to tell my dad, at this very moment, that I needed the signature of three college Deans by next week, in order to attend a Forbes Summit for young entrepreneurs, he would find a way to make it happen. Why? Because once you've witnessed someone repeatedly do amazing things, you tend to forget that even they have limitations. (I mean, Jesus walked on water, turned water into wine, fed 5,000 people with 2 fish...and people still needed to see more miracles in order to believe in him. My dad ain't the Messiah, okay?)

What I'm saying is that I have the same experiences as my brothers, only from a different angle. I could argue that because I'm his firstborn, a female in this world, and a "Daddy's Girl" at that, my pain may be deeper. I imagine how much greater my life would be if I had my dad to walk "with" me on my journey, and not just his influences. It's painful to know that someone I love and respect so deeply is so far away, and I have no answer as to how to change that reality.

To say that my siblings and I have very different relationships with my father is an understatement. All are relatively positive, but from different perspectives for sure. In my mind, I suffer from a bittersweet reality that only a daughter with a "great" absent father can relate to. Men are wired differently emotionally, and I respect that. Just don't think that you guys are alone! I strategize and shed tears routinely over the cruel reality inflicted upon the men I love, and wonder what part I can play in finding a remedy.

Over time, I have come to believe that two of my father's greatest assets are his strength and his patience. For sure we've tested his patience! Yet he allowed us to make mistakes and grow at our own pace, without holding our shortcomings against us. Even when he knew that you were going to fail at something, it's as if he calculated it into the equation and figured out how to turn it into a life lesson. I really hate that neither of my brothers took advantage of my father's keen insights, wisdom, or acute business acumen. It would have certainly made navigating life's obstacles so much easier for them. (Big facts...the lessons I learned from my dad have certainly made life easier for me!)

***

I CAN SPECIFICALLY REMEMBER a learning curve when I was in my early twenties. I guess my dad figured that he could start trusting me with his personal and business affairs. (I know, you're probably thinking that they couldn't have been that significant. You would be VERY wrong. He's incarcerated, not locked up. There's a difference!) I was handling a lot of things for him, and we developed a very trusting relationship during that time. I'll admit, I was a little lazier than he approved of, but he's from a different generation as well.

In my defense, not making an excuse, but I was young and had my eyes on the wrong prize. (At that age, we all tend to be more focused on "showing out" than truly "bossing up.") I didn't have a clue about accumulating wealth, but I would soon learn the hard lessons of real life, firsthand. My father had convinced all of his business partners and loyalists to respect the fact that I would be handling a lot more of his business from then on. Looking back at things, I can see he was making a serious shift, and certain people weren't feeling that at all. (Let's just say that my promotion put some others out of a lucrative job.) I had to learn to keep things close to the vest, as he would say. That was a good year for us financially.

I'd never had that much responsibility, and it felt good. I'd assumed that men typically groomed their sons (if they had one) to take the reins of the family empire, but he'd chosen me. That was a confidence boost for me because my father didn't deal with slouches.

I was proving to myself that I was ready to truly become a boss. Trusting me with these duties was a huge step for both of us, but by now, I knew that he was grooming me for something much bigger. As it turns out, this was also the year that we started our nonprofit organization, Anti-Bully Crusaders (ABC).

At the time, Bruh was living in the fast lane. He was cross addicted to drugs, the fast life, the women, and running with the low elements of the game. He was what I call "strung out" on life.

This lifestyle had proven to be a lethal combination for many— especially young black men. Hell, even the legends had died playing the game. It appears that Bruh got it honestly, though. According to the stories, my father had the same struggles in his teens and early twenties. From the women to the stints in jail. I had logically deduced that the system was designed to entrap generations with the same program.

Not a day goes by when I don't consider the plight of the Black men in my world. The trauma began with my dad and spread to my brothers, cousins, boyfriends, and I feared for my unborn children. I saw the smartest men manage to obtain wealth, status, and longevity, and all fell in the end. Just like my dad. It became obvious to me that the socially engineered traps were often hidden in plain sight and that even the wisest men had no answer as to how to avoid capture.

Take the justice system, for example. In some states, the law forces the jurors to simply judge innocence and guilt, but not the actual sentence. If a jury of your "peers" are NOT familiar with the actual laws, why doesn't the judge apply the law and let the peers control the sentence? Isn't it backwards? Wouldn't an educated, trained judge seem to be the likely candidate to reach the proper legal conclusion of innocence or guilt? Unless the goal is to "appear" to give the people power, while cleverly undermining their personal authority. Dictate to the people, instead of people dictating to the government. (It is "for the people, by the people," right?)

Knowing that these attitudes permeate the populace, the government has strategized to stop the common people (a jury of your peers) from deciding your punishment. Which would probably be no punishment, or a slap on the wrist. Is that the real meaning of "statutory law"? (Out of the hands of the people who supposedly decide what is appropriate? Hmmm.)

***

SO, AS STATISTICALLY PREDICTED, and proven in everyday life, my greatest fear materialized, and Bruh got locked up. He didn't do a long time, but in my mind, one day was twenty-four hours too long. I was watching the nightmare of losing my dad repeat itself right in front of my eyes. Thank God he would be home before long, I told myself.

When he got out, he convinced us all that he intended to get his life together. I knew that my parents loved this boy to death. No matter how many mistakes he made, my mother and father were always there for him. Honestly, I felt like he was my mom's favorite, because she was always harder on me. In retrospect, I was probably clueless about the worries my mom had concerning me. That was why she was so dead set against me claiming to be "in love." In her mind, that was a road to pregnancy, dependency, heartache, or potentially abuse. She was trying to help me avoid the traps that she recognized, much like my dad tried to do for my brothers.

To his credit, aside from being a hustler, Bruh was always very artistic and talented. He loved his music and technology. He was always a trendsetter, like my father. What set him apart from most young guys was that he never seemed to have an attachment to material things. I admired that.

Ultimately, Bruh decided that he wanted to attend Full Sail University in Orlando, to study music engineering. My father was gung-ho to see him in school again, but said that it cost too much at the time. While he deserved an opportunity, my dad wasn't about to roll out the red carpet and drop 80K a year, until after this fool had proven himself. That would be the equivalent of gambling a corporate salary on a historically bad decision maker. He couldn't logically justify that investment without some security. He wanted Bruh out of Texas and away from the mother of Bruh's oldest child. They had a very toxic relationship, to say the least, and she was one of the reasons that he'd gone to prison. My dad's plan to save his sons from being victims of the system depended upon breaking the chains of poisonous environments.

We all knew that if Bruh didn't get himself clean and sober, he couldn't possibly accomplish anything meaningful. He needed to have his head clear and his stuff together, or he could lose not only his freedom again, but his life. Thus, he needed a new environment where he could focus and thrive. That was the goal. I assisted by doing a little research to help my brother and dad both achieve their goals. I compiled a list of schools that my brother qualified for and were within the budget my father and I discussed. Bruh ended up choosing Atlanta Art Institute. That was perfect. He was out of Texas, which suited my dad, and he would be in school for something that he enjoyed doing. This was a best-case scenario.

In addition to those factors, the cost was more reasonable, but my dad still ended up dropping about 25K getting him set up. He needed tuition, a campus apartment, allowance, clothes, a car, a computer, and music equipment. Dad went all out for this dude.

I was really proud of Bruh and thought he was finally going to turn the corner and make something of his talents. I was there; ready to do whatever it took to see him succeed. That dream didn't last long. Two months in, this fool got kicked out for possession of not one, but two firearms and weed in his campus apartment.

While it was true that in Georgia, he had the right to possess a firearm in his home, the weed made it a felony. He didn't get charged criminally, only because there were different rules that governed campus dorms and campus apartments. Apparently he caught a break (if that's what you want to call it). He still got expelled from school.

The search and seizure were illegal as well, but I was more upset about the fact that yet another intelligent Black man had strategized to escape the trap, but was stupid enough to still act as if he lived in a war zone. Guns in college? Who does that? I thought to myself: *This dude is the luckiest, bad decision maker I know!*

My father was pissed, to say the least, but he didn't seem surprised. Again, knowing that we would fail at certain things was almost like a sixth sense for him. Was he upset that his son had failed yet again? Yes, but not "mad."

My Dad had three levels of emotional displeasure: Disappointed, Angry, and MAD! Mad was foaming at the mouth with bouts of near insanity. You didn't want to be the one to suffer the fury of his madness. I've learned that it's really hard to make him mad. I guess it's because of the catastrophic results of the bad decisions he'd made or life he'd lived in the past.

He would say: "Only a mad man gets mad and loses his mind because he's blinded in the moment by emotions that he can't control. I lost my freedom and gave up a wonderful life from being mad."

His definition of anger is a temporary state of irritation. You can still think when you're angry. "If you learn to channel your anger, it becomes an asset," he would say to me. "Anger, fueled by ambition for resolve, helps you to overcome obstacles and challenges. Every move gotta be your best move. So you gotta figure out how to move, before you move, in order to win."

I would be like, what the hell does that mean, Dad? Trust me, if you ask, he'll break it down to you and you will understand.

Disappointments were just letdowns. They were a common occurrence in life. He was fond of saying: "Expectations are at the root of all disappointment." How true! It seems that he was used to people failing him. So it didn't surprise or anger him when it happened.

"Pooh, people have a strong propensity to follow their own desires and inclinations over your objectives and goals, so when dealing with them you gotta leave room for error and compensate by having a contingency plan in place," he would say to me.

That's the reason I hated letting him down. I couldn't stomach being placed into the category of people whom he viewed as a letdown, couldn't be trusted, or were just plain stupid. My brothers are working on making that list. To make things worse, Bruh's life had begun to spiral out of control. He was making one bad decision after another. Being a ladies' man was one of his many gifts that also proved to be a curse. He could always find a random chick to take him in.

At the time, he didn't want to come home to Texas, so he stayed in Atlanta, shacking up with a girl and her mother. At this point, he was really living recklessly and without supervision. Like most people, the girl and her mom didn't care that he was smart with ambition, as long as they could benefit from his lifestyle. Before long, he was locked up for possession with intent to deliver. They left him hanging. He asked me and my mom to bond him out, but I wasn't doing anything without my dad's permission. I didn't want him mad at me. Plus it was his money that everyone wanted to use. (Again, my dad was expected to come to the rescue from prison, in another state!)

My mother could have bonded him out by herself, but she chose not to go against my father's wisdom or his wishes, either. It wasn't about the money to my dad. My brother was at the point where he had to learn a lesson or we would be responsible for enabling him to throw his life away or worse.

Dad told my mom, "Well, Kim, as long as he doesn't catch a serious case, he's gonna have to figure his life out himself."

I'm sure that this was one of the most difficult decisions my dad had ever made up till then. Here was a man, hell bent on raising his children to be healthy, independent, safe, happy, and free. He had to use logic over emotion, and it showed throughout the duration of my brother's incarceration. My dad was in constant contact with Bruh, so he wouldn't mistake tough love for abandonment. He certainly wasn't hurting for food items in jail. After leaving him there for five or six months, my mother made my father bond him out. My dad only agreed under the condition that he go to rehab in Florida. My mother thought it was a good compromise and sent me to get him.

The one thing I can say is that my brother thrives when he's sober and in a structured, positive environment around positive people. He just doesn't handle freedom very well. He doesn't have enough self-control to counteract his creative mind. This is a good reason why parents should always strive to give their children structured outlets for their energy and creativity. Isn't it apparent that A LOT of brilliant minds are in prisons, for crimes predominantly related to making money or improving a lifestyle?

As agreed upon, Bruh went to rehab in Florida. My mother set him up in one of those celebrity mansion programs. (I know...) She wanted the best for her son. I can't remember what it was exactly, but he ended up having some kind of problems down there and got kicked out of the program for a short while.

Unbelievable! This fool just can't get right, I thought to myself.

With some finessing, he managed to get a second and third chance. He finally completed the program, but this fool turned a thirty-day drug treatment program into a ninety-day experience! I was beginning to see what my father had been trying to teach us. In fact, I was learning just as much from my brother as my dad. The only difference was my brother taught me that my dad was always right. He always said that a "smart man" learns from his mistakes. A "wise man" learns from others' mistakes.

***

NO SOONER HAD MY brother been released than he and I were summoned to go visit our father. That almost didn't go so well, either. Dad was located at a prison in the Upper Peninsula of Michigan at the time. It was about a six-hour drive from our closest relatives in Flint or Detroit.

We landed at Detroit Metro Airport. I rented a car, and we went to pick up our brother DJ in Flint, before making the rest of the five-hour drive. My brothers smoked a blunt on the way. It didn't bother me. Although I don't smoke, in this hip-hop generation, everybody and their grandmother from age twelve to eighty smoked weed. We made the trip safely, and as soon as we got into the visiting room and sat down next to Pops, he was fuming with anger.

"Are you little niggaz high? What the hell is wrong with y'all? You can't go a day without getting high? Don't ever come see me high again!"

Both of my brothers just nodded in agreement, dumb looks plastered on their faces. I think my dad blew whatever high they'd had before he entered the room. I was just happy that he didn't have a reason to be angry with me. To my knowledge, I hadn't done anything.

That was the problem...I hadn't done anything! He chewed me out next.

"Pooh, you don't let these two knuckleheaded bad-decision-making fools do no thinking for you!"

I'd been sure that my dad would use me as an example of what a good offspring should be. I was shocked and felt like he was just being mean because of what my brothers had done. "But Dad—" I started to defend myself.

"But Dad, my ass! What if y'all had gotten pulled over?"

That hadn't crossed my mind.

"All these racist ass white folks up here? Or even worse—they could have taken you to jail or killed one of your dumbass brothers. Oh, what you think, they won't put your pretty little black ass in jail for being in the car with two idiots? If they put an all-American white woman like Martha Stewart in jail, your black ass don't stand a chance!" He stared me down, making me acutely aware of things that he couldn't afford to ignore.

Neither could I, for that matter. Being the oldest made me automatically responsible for my siblings. It was another one of those times when I felt like I had let my dad down, and my ego suffered for it. In this equation, I was essentially the big brother.

Even more painful was the fact that I secretly prided myself on being the smart one and I'd overlooked an important rule that he'd preached over and over: "Prevention is the key, because Damage Control is far more costly." That was only one of two mistakes. The second one was that I was about to attempt to justify my actions to a man who hated excuses. He calls it "deceptive intelligence." Essentially, you weren't smart enough to make the right decision, so you figured that being clever enough to excuse yourself was the remedy.

That logic reminds me of something I recently read: "Excuses are useless... Your friends don't need them, and your enemies don't want to hear them." My dad, being a businessman, always says: "I don't know a bank in the world where you can deposit an excuse. So I don't accept them"

That was one to grow on, and you'd be hard pressed to find another instance when my dad had to remind me of this maxim. I live by the adage that there are NO exceptions to the rules. When you make exceptions, you leave room for error. These days, we often make miscalculations..."rarely mistakes!"

Chapter Fourteen:
Trying To Understand Black Men

THERE ARE A NUMBER of reasons why I feel so strongly about culture and the relationship between Black women and Black men. For starters, we don't live in a world where we just "exist." We are constantly under scrutiny and being analyzed by other cultures and races of people. I'm only thirty-one, but until sixty-five years ago, in some states it was illegal for Whites to even marry Blacks. Maybe other cultures can't relate to the pressure of not only being a successful and responsible human, but to concurrently having your personal accomplishments measured against the accomplishments of the race as well; but I can.

That said, I realize that my struggle is only secondary to that of Black men. They are almost universally seen as hyper-aggressive and violent (except when they're needed on a playing field or boxing ring). They are viewed as criminals (except in movies that glorify ingenious criminal minds). And they are often mistrusted by Black women (who have been told that their men are "untrustworthy" by a society that hated and diminished the same men throughout history). How, then, can I not feel for my dad, my brother, my partner, or my neighbor? Even when I know that some Black men struggle to protect or respect me at times?

In his teachings, my dad attempted to give us cultural pride, while realistically warning us about people in general. He often declares his hatred and mistrust of drug users, dealers, liars, and thieves. When he first said it, I didn't get around to asking him why. I can remember thinking, *Hell, he used to sell drugs.* His comments sounded like a complete contradiction. That was part of the beauty of listening to my dad. Just when you thought you had found a chink in his armor and he didn't know it all...you found out that you were wrong! Eventually, he gave us the game.

In a nutshell, he explained that these individuals all practice a form of deception that is foremost in their characters. By trade, they cannot be trusted to put your best interest over theirs, unless you serve a greater purpose or means to a greater end. That's not to say that someone who has previously indulged in these things has become the epitome of deceptiveness or untrustworthiness. Shooting a basketball into a hoop once or occasionally doesn't make you an athlete. Do you follow the logic? He explained that when you need a drug user or dealer to come through for you, they will never fail to let you down. They are consumed with an agenda that has no room for sacrifice or selflessness. Among other things, a drug user is consumed by addiction. They are slaves to their desires. Since when does morality or the idea of wanting to be viewed as trustworthy override the desire to escape reality?

In regards to the drug dealer, haven't they already proven that the value of another life is measured by the price of a dope pack? Why then would your wellbeing change that reality? Isn't this why "making a deal" extends from drugs to police agencies when they get caught? Why do the Feds have a 96% conviction rate, with 98% of the convictions coming via plea bargain with cooperation, if dealers have such high morals? Enough said.

As for liars...they simply don't know how to be truthful. If they did, then they wouldn't be liars. The worst part is that they never consider changing the behavior that requires them to lie. The shame of their true character is such that they will never be capable of "honest" interactions. Be mindful of that. If a woman meets a man who is cheating on his girlfriend, then he is a liar. Nothing about the relationship can be based upon truth. Cheating is only cheating because of the lies. Otherwise, a man with multiple "honest" relationships is called "polyamorous," right?

In my dad's eyes, a thief is the worst of them all because his character entails all the flaws of the previous three. The act of stealing has no boundaries, as long as it satisfies the desire. Thus, a thief will steal your truth, your property, your rights, your reputation, your lover, your freedom, or your life! They have no regard for you as a person.

He emphasized this point: "Never let anyone put your freedom or life on the line for their own objectives and desires." Often, you will encounter those who want you to sacrifice your comfort or safety in the name of "friendship" or "family." Both are equally dangerous and deceptive. The proof that someone has no respect for you is evident by the fact that they will force you into circumstances that you have not chosen to participate in. Crime is an obvious one, but even a friend who would encourage you to be in an environment that clashes with your character or goals is an example. I don't know of any legitimate businessmen who just hang out in drug houses. Nor do I know any motivated people who routinely keep company with slackers.

To be clear, in today's world, not everyone who breaks the law is a criminal. Just like everyone who has worked on a car isn't a mechanic! And just because you claim to be something doesn't make you good at it either.

Often, necessity is the mother of all creativity. When we find that we need something that we don't have, we get creative. The issues arise when the options given to a certain person are limited. (I'm referencing decent people. The aforementioned kind have NO limitations on what they will employ to achieve the goal.) So the pressures from a corrupt society tend to only favor the corrupt. If left to ponder this point of view for too long without a counterbalance, one tends to succumb to the perceived necessity of breaking the rules (nice guys finish last). Are you following me?

The examples my brothers see of success, real or perceived, come from those who have taken slim odds and won. Just think...sports figures and athletes (one in how many millions make it to a professional league?), actors and TV personalities (same), famous criminals and dealers (Bernie Madoff or BMF), or even guys returning from prison to become successful (Jeremy "Jail Bae" Meeks, even Malcolm X). Thus, they are led to believe that the risks are worth the rewards. No different than the lottery. The fact that you have seen one person win reinforces the idea that you can be the one to beat the odds. Why else would so many young Black men forego an education or trade, in exchange for a dangerous wish and a prayer?

As Marsh Spears III wrote in his book *Something For Nothing Costs Way Too Much*:

Much like what we see daily, the clichés that we often repeat, begin to shape our beliefs. When your mother said that, "You can't be right and everyone else is wrong," she was unconsciously teaching you that to think outside of the norm was foolish. That is the seed of doubt that has held us back from confidently unlocking our SMART potential. Now the "machine" becomes a perpetual obstacle in your life and you feel pretty DUMB trying to ignore your parent's advice in order to do something ingenious.

I believe that the creative, individual mindset has not been propagated enough in the lives of Black men. Too few options for success are promoted. Athlete, Musician, Actor, Hustler, or Designer. Is this saying that someone who has managed to "earn" a nice living by years of hard work is less than noteworthy? Even after my father bent himself out of shape to assist my brothers, he still offered them a chance to "come up" with his help. He suggested that they and my cousins all go to barber school. Once they graduated and obtained their licenses, he offered to buy them a shop. Now, in terms of support, it doesn't get any cooler than that. A respectable family business, fully owned and staffed by blood relatives. Clearly, he just wanted to see them succeed!

Needless to say, not one of them took him up on his offer. I guess they all had better plans and opportunities. I think I'll call them and ask when is their next NBA game, sold-out concert, movie premiere, or fashion show? Yeah, right! This was just another illustration of wasted opportunity and the billion-dollar question in my mind: Why?

***

WHAT IM STILL TRYING to figure out till this day is: What in a man's DNA, or genetic makeup, allows him to ignore obvious danger and consequences, and choose extreme measures that risk

133

everything, for such small gains? Normal people would undoubtedly make the decision to go to school, get a job, and live a low-risk, law abiding life (as opposed to dangerous, short-term crime). My father is not excluded from the "abnormal" thinkers. Nor does my love and admiration for him absolve him from the bad decisions he made, which cost our family so much!

The mystery of this psychology gets deep. I wonder if it's true that if you tell someone they're ugly or worthless enough times that they'll start to believe it. Clearly, society plays a role in self-esteem. Who can deny that stereotypes permeate the collective minds of common people? If you disagree, or are unwilling to admit your own prejudices, let's play a game of word association:

If a Black man is the richest person in a room full of successful Whites, what does he do for a living? (The key words are "Black" and "Successful.") Do you automatically think entertainer or athlete? If you don't, you are in a very small class of people who don't associate Black success with "anything outside of education."

Let's try the word "Professor." Who automatically comes to mind? (White man?) Let's use the word "Doctor." Does an Indian or foreigner come to mind? (Or someone White?) What about "gas station owner"? (Let's be honest...Middle Easterner?)

Let's try something different and not categorize careers, but regions. Let's try "Suburban." (White, right?) "Ghetto?" (Black?) Okay..."Private school?" Or something as obscure as "the solarium" in my friend's house? Who are the last people who come to mind? I might even agree that Black people are the last to have a solarium in their home. We are all ignorant of things beyond our experience.

The point that I'm making is that I cannot simply attribute the reckless decision-making of my father and the men I have encountered for most of my life to "stupidity." Some of these men epitomize the word "ingenious." Most have, at some time or another, managed to accumulate a respectable degree of wealth from the worst conditions: the worst educational systems, the worst home environments, and a terrible assembly of associates and employees. So, in my estimation, they are far from stupid.

***

THE NEXT THING TO consider is that one can only teach what they know. I didn't personally experience being punished with switches and extension cords, but my dad and uncles all talk about this form of corporal punishment being the norm, just a generation earlier. My father grew up in a different era of discipline that gave him a different perspective on what constitutes pain or fear. His father, my grandfather, LeRoy (T-Roy) Washington, Sr., was a war veteran and a hard-working, ex-military man. He rarely used violence with my dad, but he was strict. That was something taught to my dad, and it's part of his makeup till this day. However, my Great-granny Copeland, my dad's grandmother, was a Christian woman who did not hesitate to mete out physical violence as a way

135

of correction. She was a true provider and matriarch. At one time, nineteen people lived in her house.

My dad and uncles lived with his granny during their adolescent days. Her rule was that EVERYBODY had to attend church. A feat that required three car trips to accomplish, with kids sitting on each other's laps. You have to hear my dad tell the story. Her ritual, according to my dad, was to cook a big Sunday breakfast, feed everyone, and then pile up for the long Sunday service that didn't end until the afternoon.

One day when he was nine years old, my dad decided that he wasn't going to church. It was too boring for him. He used the excuse that he and my uncle Boo were Muslim and that church was for Christians. His grandmother told him that he was going to church, and if he didn't shut his mouth and eat, he would be going to church hungry. At this part of the story, my dad likes to say that he made the fatal mistake that got him slapped into "Hell." Feeling frustrated that his logic hadn't gotten him an excused absence from church, he stomped his foot and yelled out that he didn't even believe in GOD. (Yeah, I'm thinking just what you are...)

The next thing my dad remembered was waking up to seeing flames burning inches away from his face and feeling the heat on his skin. It was clear that he had been sent to Hell for his sins. He concluded that God had struck him down for saying that he didn't believe in him. Certainly, he believed in God. He'd just been running his mouth. At that moment, he wanted to tell God that he was sorry and hoped that he could have his life back.

In actuality, what had occurred was that as soon as he made the statement, my great-grandmother slapped him so hard that she knocked him unconscious, and he fell onto the kitchen floor. In those times, they had the stoves with a tray beneath the oven that was used for toasting bread or broiling food. He'd awakened to see the flames from the oven's open flap and concluded that he was in Hell.

By the time he regained enough consciousness to realize that he was laid out on the kitchen floor, he was being ordered to get into the car for church. Needless to say, that was a traumatic experience for a nine-year-old child, but it became a source of humor later in life. When I hear those stories, it explains some things that I readily diagnose as part of the reason my generation seems to be so out of control.

***

IT'S APPARENT TO ME that a lot of our men have been raised without fathers, or with fathers who can only teach from a traumatized mindset. They don't know how to promote normalcy or teach the principles of it, as it relates to certain things. Not that I have the answer in its entirety; but clearly part of the problem is they haven't been taught life should ultimately be a pleasurable experience. Thus, they view the dangers associated with attempting to change this reality not to be much of a factor. As my brothers and cousins would say about getting in trouble, "An Ass whipping is an ass whipping Might as well make it worth it."

In my feminine mind, that was the dumbest thing I ever heard. Why not just refrain from doing it? On the other hand, I have sometimes wished that I had the courage to try some of the things that they got away with (can't lie). But common reasoning dictates that I could never be comfortable risking my health, my life, or my freedom for trinkets...or private jets and millions, either.

My dad's analogy is a lot more cut and dried. He attributes the behavior to "males" not being shown the example from real "men." He says that someone has to love them and have the knowledge of how to teach them the principles of manhood. This will allow them to choose to become men. Some will still choose to be weak, but most will follow the examples of how to become mature men. He told me the story of a Hindu village that worshipped elephants. The people allowed the elephants free rein and considered them welcome guests. They even fed the elephants better than they fed their children, because they saw them as gods.

One year, poachers killed off all of the adult bull elephants for their ivory tusks. They only left two small males who had not grown tusks. In the days that followed, the young male elephants began to run wildly and ravage the town, terrorizing the people. The villagers couldn't understand why. Attempting to understand, the townspeople captured the events on video and sent it to an African elephant conservationist. Upon seeing the contents of the video, the zoologist said, "I know exactly what's wrong." He shipped two adult bull elephants to the village. Initially, the younger elephants clashed with the new adult males. However, within a week or so, the less experienced males deferred to the adults and followed the pecking order. The next time the people saw the elephants roaming through the village, the younger elephants were calmly following the herd and behaving perfectly.

The moral of the story is that the younger elephants didn't know how to behave like adults because all of the adult examples were gone. "Pooh, the same is taking place with our youth today. Most of the men who can demonstrate the example of true manhood are either preoccupied, in prison, or deceased. Those who are in society are predominantly concerned with the hustle and bustle of daily life, or just not concerned with our youth. The rest are downright losers with nothing to offer! This forces the younger generation to lean on their own knowledge and learn from those who are just as unqualified as they are. The failing justice system is a microcosm of our failing society. The blind are leading the blind and ignorant leadership is perpetuating itself rapidly."

Following his eloquent analysis, I don't think my father had any idea of how disheartened I was to know that once again, he was right.

***

ALL OF MY BIOLOGICAL and extended family of uncles are manly men. My father and all of my uncles were fortunate to have fathers in the household, as well as a lot of brothers and cousins to help raise them. It's unquestionable that most of them were major players in their younger years: handsome, street smart guys, athletic and very popular. Obviously, my mother and her sisters couldn't get enough of these men. They each married into the circle of friends. These guys were raised like a village, a crew, a FAMILY! They had each other's back's, loved each other, went to school together, hustled together, lived together, kicked ass together, went to the extremes for one another, and some even went to prison together and never sold one another out (BIG facts!). In fact, most of them did a stint and came home to get their lives on track. Those who didn't fall into the trap were wise enough, or fortunate enough, to escape the streets, eventually.

My uncle Pruitt, who was killed in 2012, was the last one to have one foot in and one foot out. That loss devastated my father because he felt he was a bad influence on his younger brother when they were coming up. At the time, their sense of manhood was directly connected to their ability to provide "by any means." Poverty was a disease, in which the poison of crime seemed preferable.

I'm proud of my uncles for changing their lives; none of them are in the streets anymore. Don't get me wrong. They still have street ties. They have family and friends who refuse to change. But hell, we all do. Just don't make the mistake that might necessitate calling on that branch of the family tree!

As I compare my brothers from this generation to my dad and uncles, you can see a stark difference. Not only are the mannerisms different, but what influences and drives them is different as well. The desire to own something that can be passed down through generations doesn't seem to be the goal anymore.

Though times have definitely changed, the characteristics and traits of successful people are the same in any era. The principles of integrity or the rules that only the most disciplined and focused adhere to are the determining factor: On the other hand, there has been a perpetual theme from a dark past that serves as a common denominator in the decay and demise of the Black family unit. The men are somehow removed from the equation. First it was slavery; now it's the penal system (modern day slavery). Even the laws or journalistic media will often blatantly promote the idea that the manly duties and responsibilities to the family unit can be better accomplished by women. As a result, the women who buy into this ideology or face the brute reality are forced to support the family alone. They must now chase a better job, a wealthy benefactor, or hustle in order to survive. In an attempt to create better opportunities for themselves, many have relocated to other parts of the country in search of stability.

This further contributes to the breaking up of the family unit and the respect factor between the sexes. How long did it take for the general consensus of Black women to go from: "Looking for tall, dark, and handsome" to "I don't need a man?" I'm not sure if this was coincidentally or by design, but I do know the effect it has had on young Black men! They now view relationships with Black women as a battle. We are either weak and lazy, or masculine and disrespectful (to the vast majority of men).

As with the story of the Hindu Village, the young bulls have been left to figure out manhood on their own. That has led them to often imitate this fictitious lifestyle, promoted by music and television, to gauge what a man is, or isn't. This fallacy has perpetuated a dog-eat-dog mentality and glorified the killer mindset. Mostly for cheap, material trinkets. The sad thing about it is that we ultimately have no one to blame but ourselves.

As a collective, we've moved away from the basic humanity of loving one another and promoting a sense of community. We have stopped putting the welfare of others high on our priority list. Instead we have become socially and culturally poor "elitists," who judge one another based upon image instead of character. Everything is about self-preservation, or self-glorification. When you can only rise as high as an individual, then you can never really see the concept of teamwork for the family unit.

While there are a lot of external factors that contribute to these conditions, it doesn't absolve my father's generation for the role they played in the demise of the men in my generation. Nor do the men in my generation get a pass for their irresponsible behavior. At some point, our men must rise above the obstacles they face and be more than the moment suggests. Mediocrity can no longer be the new "excellence." The stakes are too high and the cost is too extreme. One mistake can destroy your life and the lives of your children as well. And for what? The fleeting, momentary satisfaction of immediate gratification? How many of our people have died or been sent to prison for these misguided truths? We have so much more value and potential. We must become the MASTERS OF OUR OWN DESTINY!

Chapter Fifteen:
People Must Be Reevaluated

LEY ARRIVED IN MARCH. We found a high-rise apartment and signed a one-year lease. It was all fun and adventure as she and I were getting settled into our new apartment. In true Diva mode, she had her Lexus coupe delivered, so the city knew she had arrived. We both decided we should purchase all new furnishings. Neither of us wanted anything to remind us of our old relationships. "New lives, new beginnings" was our mutual mantra.

I spent the next week showing her around town and introducing her to some of my associates who would soon become her circle as well. Being a somewhat accomplished and motivated young woman, she fit right in with the group.

To anyone watching, I guess you could say that we were living our best lives, while becoming reacquainted. You should have seen all the attention we got when we went out.

Ley had really grown up and become edgier than I remembered her being. A savage slickness about herself. She was ruthless with men: used them like boys and discarded them like toys. I always wondered, had the military and traveling abroad done this to her, or had some traumatic life experience occurred after we parted ways?

I made a mental note that lying and deceiving came easily for her. But I guess that as long as it came at another's expense and we benefitted from it, she could be the bad girl if she wanted to. I told myself that that part of her life wasn't my business. Although I worried about her, my motto was, "No harm, no foul." She was making the game work for her. I was taught to never hate on anybody's come up.

After getting settled in, the first thing Ley wanted to do was plan a girls' trip out of the country. I hadn't been abroad since my sixth-grade honors class visited Europe. It seemed so long ago, but I could still remember it like it was yesterday. It felt like a constant reminder that time was flying by, and I still hadn't accomplished any of my goals. In fact, at that time, I still hadn't figured out how I was even going to reach them. My dad's words: "Time waits for nobody" would echo in my head daily. Ley's idea to visit somewhere exotic made me consider that maybe we owed it to ourselves. I was game, and it didn't take much to convince the other girls. Neha already had a valid passport, I had to renew mine, and Paris had to apply for one. Ley was traveling on her military ID.

Of all the places in the world to see, Ley chose Medellin, Colombia. South America? I was thinking: *Isn't that like a third-*

world country ran by the cartel? Why would she want us to go there? It could be dangerous and we could get kidnapped. All type of things were going through my mind. The military had turned Ley into G.I. Jane. I was a little more reserved. I had plans for all the things I wanted to do in life. I had no desire to live fast and die young! I'd seen other people go out like that, and it was the stuff of my nightmares. So yes, I was a little afraid.

To add to my worries, even if I survived the trip, my parents would probably kill me when I got back. I definitely couldn't tell them where I was going beforehand. That would have certainly been met with an, "Are you out of your f@#king mind?" My dad would have shut it down for everyone. He would have been using his secret underworld connects to get the phone numbers to parents he hadn't even met. So we all concocted the story that we were going on a work-related trip to the Bahamas with Neha.

Typically, I never lie to my parents. We have a strict code about that. I told myself that it was a partial truth, so it didn't feel like a complete betrayal of the trust. We were actually going to spend the last three days of a ten-day trip in the Bahamas. We agreed to accompany Neha to the set where one of her company's artists would be shooting a music video. What the hell, you only live once. Plus, I consciously lived by the rules that my dad had embedded in me over the years. Never leave your food or drink unattended. Don't count on someone else to watch it for you. Never allow anyone to

146

convince you to carry anything in your bags for them. Especially a dude. Always check your luggage thoroughly. You are solely responsible for its contents. You can't trust nobody! Never pull out large amounts of cash. Stay together in a group; it's safer. Never get drunk or experiment with drugs. Someone might lace your stuff! Drink unopened bottled water, and whenever possible buy your liquor unopened and drink in your room. Never in public. Never venture outside the tourist area in other countries. Stay away from the hood when traveling to other places. It's far too dangerous! I got it, Dad!

Those standards had become a part of my natural process by then. I knew what was up. However, the girls already had me breaking rule #1: "Never lie to my parents!"

For the trip, our itinerary was completely planned out to the max. It turned out that Colombia was far more beautiful than I ever imagined it to be. The five of us shared a large suite in a five-star hotel, and the food was really good. Everything was all paid for, courtesy of one of Ley's sponsors. We frequented the nearby tourist attractions and visited a coffee bean farm. It turned out that Ley's benefactor was a wealthy businessman. He was buying the farm (literally), and Ley was there to take pictures and get the logistics of how the business operated.

She spoke with the owner in his native tongue and I was like, "Where in the hell did she learn that?" Surprisingly, we found out later that in the military she had been a professional translator. She spoke a number of languages, including French, German, Korean, Spanish, and Portuguese. Fluently.

My girl was killing two birds with one stone: bonding with the girls on vacation and doing business. She was on her A-game! I found it inspirational to see one of us living life to the fullest. My girl was not afraid to travel the world, meet people, and make investments into the future. She was getting her grown woman on, and I was motivated to follow suit.

On the last day of the trip, we planned a helicopter ride over the city. The aerial view gave us a glimpse into the parts of the town that we didn't get to visit. We flew over the poorest part of the city and saw an area known as a "shanty town." To say that it would be uninhabitable for most people in the civilized world would be an understatement. The construction of the makeshift homes seemed to be a sparse collection of tin or aluminum sheets, old wooden doors, and planks, fastened together by rope, nails, and hope. The dirt paths that ran between the dwellings appeared to be made by heavy rains and foot traffic. There was trash and debris everywhere. Hand-washed clothes hung from lines, and kids and wild animals could be seen digging and playing in the same trash heaps. I couldn't imagine anything but the stench of poverty and despair emanating from below. It almost made me cry. I couldn't imagine anyone living like that. It had the most humbling effect on me and immediately redefined what I thought of as hard times.

We'd never seen anything like this in America. It did two things to me: It made me more grateful for what I had; and it made me want to go harder in life, so I could help even more people. I wanted to visit the town right then, but the tour guide told me that it was strictly prohibited. While there were a lot of nice people who would welcome us, there were far more gangs and kidnappers who wouldn't hesitate to ransom us for American Dollars. The tour guide validated my father's biggest fears about us traveling abroad, and now I saw what he was talking about firsthand.

To hell with what my girls were talking about! This could have gone really badly for us. Do you remember what happened to those Black people in Mexico in early 2023? After seeing the shanty town, I vowed that for the rest of my life, I would be more conscious of everything around me. I couldn't stop thinking about the movie *Taken*. If something had happened to us, my dad was not a Special Ops agent. He was locked up and he definitely wasn't coming to save us.

We flew back to Miami, met up with Neha's people, and jumped on a chartered flight (all courtesy of the label). This was my first time going to the Bahamas or flying on a private jet. I wasn't a ghetto girl, but I wasn't uppity or bourgeois, either. I had flown first class, but it was nothing like "private jet" first class...and for FREE!

After flying commercial for my whole life, I now understood why the rich needed the luxury of their own private planes. It made traveling easy and fun. Who had time to be waiting in lines when there were deals to be made, right? That became another experience that fueled my ambitions. When I accomplished my goals and became super-successful, that would be the only way to travel.

As we arrived and prepared to land, I could see the aqua blue water and the lush tones of the island. The view was so beautiful from the air. My mind instinctively envisioned the day when I could share this feeling with my dad. I felt the pangs of sorrow for all the years he'd been deprived of the freedom to spread his wings and come and go as he pleased. The sadness from my realization of his decades in prison nearly made me shed a tear, but he would never approve of me showing weakness on his behalf in front of anyone, so I held my composure.

Neha had reserved a villa at a resort for us. Our first night on the island, we attended a formal industry dinner. It appeared that no one else had invited family or friends. Neha didn't care what anyone else did. She brought us because she was a boss like that. I guess that growing up rich gave her the "I don't need you, you need me!" attitude.

We soon learned that Neha wasn't just an intern. She had written the treatment for the video and was co-directing the shoot. It didn't surprise me at all.

She spent nearly twelve hours on the set for the next two days. All the while, she spared no expense in planning a fun weekend for us while she worked. The girls and I went parasailing, zip-lining, scuba diving, jet skiing, and shopped nonstop! The only time we saw Neha was for the label's showcase on a private yacht.

The day before we were set to depart, we were so exhausted that all we could do was rest. We had all tried to stuff a few years' worth of adventure into two days. None of us even had the energy to leave the room for dinner. That included Neha, "the Energizer Bunny," and Ley, who was "Miss Adventure." Instead, we lay around in our PJs and ordered room service from breakfast to dinner.

I used the time to reflect on my own life. Sitting quietly by the pool, I asked myself, "How am I gonna find a sustainable hustle? Something that will take me to the next level?" After experiencing such a lavish weekend with my girls, there was no way I could be satisfied with a normal, mundane life ever again. I had been awakened to what I was missing out on and what the benefits of hard work should look like. My goals had gone from simply wanting to have money to needing the financial freedom to live large! There was a huge difference.

***

THE LAST LEG OF the trip took us back to Atlanta, where we stayed the night, before heading in our respective directions. That night, we went downtown for drinks and steak dinners. We started playing an 80s retro tabletop game called *Pac Man*. We all reveled in the excitement of trying to outdo one another's high score as we were chased around by the ghosts while trying to clear the maze. During the height of the excitement, one of the girls came up with the idea that we should give our crew a name.

Paris was the one to say, "It's obvious that we should call ourselves 'The Ghost Pac' because this game represents our lives. We're like the Ghost chasing the yellow muncher that represents chasing our dreams, racing around the maze and obstacles of life."

I don't know if it was because we'd had a few drinks, but Paris could be deep like that at times. "The Ghost Pac it is!" we all agreed. We all took one last drink, toasted to a wonderful vacation of work and play, and took a vow to honor the pact for life.

"Like Bad Boys...We ride together, we die together. Ghost Pac for life!"

As we left, we happened to walk past a tattoo shop that seemed to have been built since we entered the bar, because no one noticed it when we arrived. Ley said, "Let's get Ghost tats." Everyone looked at one another and simultaneously replied, "Let's do it." Before we had a chance to reconsider, we were inside. Each girl picked a different color ghost to represent something about herself. I chose red because my life had been a rollercoaster of ups and downs. I was thinking of my renewed determination to succeed after seeing the shanty town, and the red ghost represented the fire I felt to level up and match the energy of my girls.

The red ink on my skin was a constant reminder of my burning desire to chase down life and TAKE my piece of the American Dream. The urge to do something major for myself, my family, and the man who had given me all the necessary tools to be a giant. My dad. The Ghost Pac was born out of this adventurous moment and was a declaration to be a powerhouse team, chasing success and loyalty for life!

***

AFTER SPENDING A COUPLE of weeks escaping life and forging bonds with my crew, it was time to go home and face the music. I don't know what anyone else was thinking, but in that moment of silence when your true reality catches up with you, all I could think was, *How am I gonna tell my parents where I have been?*

The dishonesty would eat at me if I didn't. On top of that, rent was due in another week, and I had to figure out how to balance my responsibilities with all the money I had splurged on traveling. I still hadn't found a sustainable hustle, and it was a reminder that my life was a hot mess!

As I anticipated, my mother didn't trip too hard when I confessed. She was just happy that we made it back safely. She still admonished me to never leave the city, let alone the country, without letting her know where I was going, ever again.

"If it's your dad you're worried about, then you're right. He needs to know where you're going too," she concluded, then asked me to see the pictures.

I would be lying to say that I didn't know my dad would be livid when he found out about the actual destination of the trip. He caught me and Ley together and laid into us hard! I kind of liked when my dad checked us all together. For some reason it made me feel like we were sharing a ritualistic part of my life. Sometimes it was funny. At other times it wasn't. It didn't matter which of us had said or done whatever my dad disagreed with. "That was the dumbest shit I've ever heard" or "What made you do that dumb ass shit?" was his response.

He'd let us have it with no filter. He was just that kind of man.

I have to make a mental note to ask him how each dumb thing we did could end up being dumber than the "dumbest shit he ever heard" previously? One thing was for sure, if I said or did anything that didn't make sense, he'd be the one to chew my head off for real.

This time, Ley attempted to step up and take the brunt of the admonishment for me.

"Dad, it was my fault. I asked all the girls to go on this business trip with me," she explained, hoping to have a calming effect. She went on to explain that she had previously been to Colombia on a few occasions and that it was honestly a business move. He still didn't relent. He held his ground. His fatherly instincts and

154

dominance had a way of making all the girls act as if they were his daughters as well.

I think that in a world full of timid or weak-minded men with no solid constitution, they had an appreciation for his candidness. He'd give you a chance to explain; then he'd always give you a better solution or method. They felt like he understood them.

Absolutely doing the most and trying to save face in front of Ley, I let yet another dumb statement come out of my mouth: "I'm grown and I don't need your or Mama's permission to—"

He shut me down mid-sentence. "PERMISSION?" his voice boomed through the phone. "Let me tell you something, grown ass woman. I don't give a damn how grown you get. As long as you're alive, you'll be my child! You don't get to leave the country without our knowing or getting our PERMISSION!"

This time he was mad.

"Do you understand?"

"Yes, Dad," was all I could muster.

So much for trying to show out in front of Ley. She looked at me with her lips twisted and her hands in the air, as if to ask me: "What the fuck?" I immediately realized that I should have just kept my mouth shut. I knew that I wasn't going to get away with back-talking my dad. He hated that with a passion, and I honestly don't know what I was thinking.

"Listen," he said, making both Ley and me look at one another with worry. We knew that it was coming!

"Look, ladies, it's because you're grown that I expect more out of you. As you grow, so does my expectation that you have the ability to discern. Y'all smart, but sometimes you too smart for your own good. I'm pissed, but not because you left the country or you're handling business. I'm pissed because you know better than to leave without telling us." He added in a calm, cool voice, "And if you're not consulting with me on something, it's because you know it's something I might not agree with. That's a form of deception."

I don't know how he's able to switch gears like that. It keeps you on edge, but even if you're bearing the brunt of his tongue lashing, you're still anticipating what he has to say next. We instinctively knew that by the time he was done talking, we would have learned something valuable that we could use down the line. It was an effective skill that I wanted to acquire. The bottom line was that ultimately, he was right, and we knew it.

In most instances, even if he didn't agree with our choices, he would allow us to make our own mistakes as long as we put safety first. Everyone should know that you definitely need a security plan in place when leaving the country, right?

***

NOT LONG AFTER WE arrived back home, Ley asked me to fly out to NYC for a meeting with her attorneys. Apparently, she'd had a very serious accident while on the job in the military that left her with some type of brain damage. When she told me the story, I felt bad for her, but at the same time, I was so grateful to God that I had never experienced anything as traumatic as that.

We arrived at a high-rise in downtown Manhattan and took the elevator up to the 47th floor. Everything about the firm spoke of money. BIG MONEY! The luxurious polished redwood furnishings were separated by wall-to-wall glass. They even had a catered buffet in their personal lobby for their employees and clients.

After about twenty minutes, Ley was called into a conference room, alone. A well-dressed receptionist directed me to a more comfortable, private waiting area. It appeared to be an employees' lounge. It was equally opulent and awe-inspiring. I sat facing the office that Ley had been taken to, and I could see her through the glass, sitting with her back to me. There appeared to be two attorneys, and a younger woman sitting at the edge of the table taking notes. Never one to sit idle, I figured that I could kill two birds with one stone and popped open my laptop to get some work done. The amazing thing about moments like these is that you almost always meet someone you can add to your Rolodex. Employees of the firm were coming in and out of the lounge area regularly. Almost everyone who entered into the room immediately introduced themselves and asked me the same questions:

"Are you new?"

"Who are you interning for?"

I guess the attire and laptop suggested "lawyer" rather than "secretary." I had several great conversations. Needless to say, I never got to the work I was planning on doing, but I made two mental notes: I had to get my business vernacular up, and I needed to travel with business cards. Both would strengthen my position, or at least make people take me more seriously.

Ley finally emerged from the office with a smirk on her face. I looked at my watch and noticed that an hour and a half had gone by really fast. She remained silent until we got on the elevator and then explained how the law firm was trying to settle her case for $700,000, but she wanted $3 million.

"Those blood drinking lawyers are gonna get a third of my money," she spat with disgust, and then added, "At least I convinced them to give me a $300,000 advance. I just gotta wait ninety days to get the damn money!"

I didn't know what her ailments were, or the physical and mental pain she suffered, but otherwise she seemed to be perfectly normal to me.

I was thinking, *Three hundred grand is a pretty good lick, and they will still owe her some bread? Put me up on game!*

***

IN LESS THAN A week, Ley had a fresh one on the line. One of our associates introduced her to a guy, and before you knew it, he was sprung! It didn't surprise me. Ley was what you call a real Bad B#%ch! She was a triple threat: Fine, had money, and was educated. But things weren't quite adding up. When rent came, she asked me to cover her half until she and ol' boy got back from New York. I didn't think anything of it at the time. I told her that I would cover this month's rent and she could just cover next month. To be honest, I really didn't have it to spare and almost asked why she didn't just wire it to me. But I knew that my girl had paper and it wouldn't be any issues with getting my money back. She was only gone for five days, and when she got back, she gave me half of the rent and bills and the next month's as well. She was even talking about upgrading her car.

That was all the proof I needed to rest assured that the delay was a one-time thing for her. I figured that she'd gotten the 300 g's while in New York, but she didn't say anything, so I didn't ask. I knew better than to step out of my lane when it came to other people's money, because I hate when people try to count mine.

A couple months prior, I had made the mistake of telling Ley how I got my car and a few dollars. The excitement of having my sister back in my life loosened my lips and made me overfamiliar, way too soon. My father always taught me that loose lips sink ships. "Never expose to anyone how you made your money, and especially don't introduce them to your plug or clientele. That amateur move is an invitation to get 'backdoored' for your hustle. If someone has that crucial information, they certainly don't need you anymore. On top of that, you run the risk of them being better at the hustle than you are. Now you have to figure out a new way to eat."

I asked Tee if I could introduce her to Ley and a few of our people. She reluctantly agreed. For some reason, she never really liked Ley or any of my supposed friends. She always tried to tell me that they were jealous of me. I dismissed it as her not really knowing our history and how close we were as teenagers. Plus, I was living a mediocre life, struggling to pay bills and in a relationship that was pushing me to the edge. Why would anyone be jealous of that?

I don't know if it was because she was so much older than us, or if her motherly instincts always allowed her to see what I couldn't. What I did know was, there were two undeniable things about Tee: She was a beautiful woman inside and out, and if you were on her team she would give you the shirt off her back. She always pushed me to be the best version of myself. She would always say things like, "If I knew back when I was your age the things I know now... You need to use your real talents... Listen to your father, he knows what he's talking about," etc.

Like most people I introduced to my dad, Tee had a great deal of reverence for his and my relationship. He always liked Tee as well. Over time, they developed a nice, respectful acquaintance.

I think that having a daughter and family members depending on her at such an early age robbed her of her dreams. At this point in her life, she figured she could teach me a few things and live on through me. In a way, she reminded me of my parents, and I feel honored that she saw something in me that endeared me to her. That was no small matter to me.

The other thing that I love and admire about Tee is that she's not only smart and independent, she's also well connected. She knew some of everybody...doctors, lawyers, business owners, bankers...butchers, bakers, and candlestick makers!

My dad always says: "It's not what you know, it's who you know. Your network is your net worth!"

Through them, I learned and now understand how important it is to be well-connected. You gotta know somebody who knows somebody! In order to level up, you have to run into someone who knows more than you and be a fast learner and innovator.

***

LEY HAD AN 800 credit score. The only other person I ever met who had a perfect score was my grandmother (my dad's mother). With a military background and consistent income, it was going to be easy for her to get any type of financial package she desired. I made it clear that she was going to have to give Tee a kickback. For some reason, I just felt like I had to tell her that.

She hadn't crossed any of the circle, but her moves were a little questionable, and I needed to protect Tee. She was a godsend and my family at this point. My dad and Granny always said, "Business is business." And even when it's not a strictly business relationship, we still break bread, because it's an honorable way to show our appreciation. You would be surprised how many partnerships are made or broken by that small gesture. In my dad's old line of work, even if your brother got you on with his connect with no tax; you "tipped" him to show appreciation. That ensured that if you ever needed him again, he wouldn't feel slighted by the last deal. That was something I'd come to put into my repertoire, automatically.

With Tee's direction, Ley filled out all the paperwork and easily qualified for a $50,000 business loan, $50,000 personal loan, and $50,000 line of credit. In addition, they financed her car, approved a $25,000 credit card, and she prequalified for a $400,000 veteran's first-time home buyers loan. It was unbelievable how much money they were willing to give her. Last I knew, we were high school students, essentially in the same financial boat. Now, she was stunting and all I could think was, *Damn, I gotta get my credit right!*

I'm a risk taker. If I had her opportunity, my "go-for-the-gold" personality would have made me take all of that money. It wasn't like the bank was going to send Pookie, Earl, and Ray Ray to come collect if you didn't pay on time. Ley, on the other hand, was better with money than I was. My dad tried to convince her to take the home loan, purchase a property in North Dallas, and lease it out for passive income until our lease was up, and then move out there. At the time, interest rates were fair, and it was a buyer's market. She declined, and I was disappointed that all my credit mistakes didn't allow me to capitalize on the moment. Nonetheless, I was happy for my girl. She only took the credit card and financed her car...or so I thought.

Chapter Sixteen:
Dads Business Rules 101

"It's not your job to reinvent the wheel. It's your job to improve the wheel. If you don't have a new invention, service, or product, you hustle off the hustle, or become a disruptor."

IKNOW YOU'RE THINKING, *What does that mean?* Let me give you the game the way it was given to me. Firestone or Goodyear didn't invent the tire. Through innovation and evolution, they've continuously found a way to make it better. While the wheel has evolved from stone to steel, so has the tire—from solid rubber, inflated, steel-belted, and now run-flat tires that will maintain their integrity for more than fifty miles with a hole the size of a quarter drilled into it. The point is that innovation and evolution often trump creating something new. So, as written in *Something For Nothing...*:

An intelligent business mind will see the potential to find a peripheral angle where you may "attach" yourself to a profitable division of a market that has already been created for you. Sort of like selling pans, picks, and shovels to gold miners. The miners may not get rich, but the person selling them tools of the trade will definitely prosper.

Do you think Bill Gates considered the emotions of his friends at Microsoft or IBM when he designed the Windows program and disrupted the PC industry? His software invention forced the PC (personal computer) industry to essentially succumb to his model. At one point, every PC in the world needed his Windows program to function. If a company's PC was incompatible with his system, their computers were considered obsolete. This is also an example of disrupting an industry by attaching yourself to a pre-existing business. The fact that he was accused of monopolizing the market and intentionally violating Sherman Anti-trust laws only validated the effectiveness of his approach.

Likewise, Steve Jobs and Apple didn't invent the cellphone. I'm pretty sure that it was What'sHisFace, right? Exactly my point! Often, an inventor of a product does not see the innovative changes that can drive even larger sales. In turn, someone else benefits as much (or more) because of small innovations. That's where we come in.

For the savvy street hustler, allow me to give a relatable example for you as well. According to my dad, in the 80s (naturally, before I was born), the crack epidemic hit our neighborhoods hard. In many respects, we still haven't recovered from the residual effects. However, that's a conversation for another time and place.

Unfortunately, the tons of cocaine that hit the streets awakened the entrepreneurial spirit in some people. While many lost their dignity and personal constitution to addiction, others saw opportunity.

Many of the unsuccessful peddlers lost their lives or went to prison for a very long time. However, many large corporations and legitimate businessmen got rich from this tragedy, with no risk involved. Seizing the opportunity, they sold legal paraphernalia: scales, baggies, pipes, baking soda, Pyrex measuring cups, etc.— items that were considered illegal to possess, according to ambiguous laws, but not illegal to sell. (Don't ask me!) Then came the marijuana pandemic that followed in the 1990s-2000s. The cigar manufacturers and their shareholders benefitted from a new kind of weed smoker. Smoking "blunts" had the unintended (or very intentional) effect of making people cross-addicted. Smoking weed in nicotine leaves promoted this passive addiction. Most still believe till this day that they just like the way the tobacco leaves "make the weed taste." Hmmm? Unsurprisingly, those same people are loyal customers at hookah bars (flavored tobacco) today.

Marijuana has been legalized in most states, and still tobacco thrives. It's apparent that only the outliers will seized the opportunity there, as well.

The bottom line is this: The concept of business is the same all across the board. You find a service or product that is in demand, legitimize it, buy it low, sell for a profit, and pay your taxes! If you happen to fall into the small percentage of those who can invent something that no one else has thought of, same process, except you don't have to purchase from someone else. I am always fascinated by how great minds operate similarly. I was recently speaking with one of my business associates and mentors, J.C.Williams. He's old school like my dad and a good friend of the family. He has an interesting analogy of how he sees an opportunity to be a disruptor in the business world.

He said, "Lauren, close your eyes and imagine a forest. If it was all yours, what would be the most beautiful part of that?" I was thinking of a beautiful horizon where the sun was rising or setting. He must have realized that I was daydreaming and added, "For a business opportunity."

I immediately replied, "Lumber."

He replied, "Everyone sees something different. Firewood, furniture, paper, etc. The difference with people like your dad and me is that we think, 'Why compete when you can own the market?' You know what I see?"

"What?" I asked, knowing that I was about to learn something. (I am always hungry to learn useful and valuable lessons from professionals. Especially for free. These men typically get paid for their game.)

He said, "I see a googleplex of toothpicks. Millions of trillions of them. I see me disrupting the market by cutting the price of a box of 100 toothpicks and forcing every restaurant, martini bar, or wholesaler to buy them from me. That's market disruption!"

While he wasn't serious about toothpicks, or looking to buy a forest, it was the science that was important. That conversation helped me to look at every commercial, movie, webinar, or lecture differently. Now, I'm looking for the angle or the benefit to me. How can I innovate or disrupt an industry? Can I buy into a soft drink brand, use my celebrity influence to call basic Kool-Aid "Diet Water," and sell it for billions? Hell, it worked for 50 Cent.

One thing is for sure, I will never look at a treeline the same way again!

***

AT THIS STAGE OF life, I was ready to take the game by storm with ABC. Ley and I had finally gotten settled in, and I was thinking: *It's time to figure out how to scale our project.* I was thinking of getting the Nobel Peace Prize for Humanitarian Efforts for Change. Clearly, the change Ley had in mind was a monetary upgrade, and I wasn't mad at her.

My father always said that if you find something you love to do and improve the process so it's more efficient or cutting edge, the money will follow. I believed that, even if no one else did.

I won't lie... It still hurt a little to realize that everything was on me again. Good thing I didn't understand the degree of difficulty the journey would entail. I've heard people say that ignorance is bliss. I had no idea that I would soon have a reality check.

Chapter Seventeen:
People Should Be Reevaluated, Part 2

T HE GIRLS' REUNION IN Atlanta had been the catalyst to what I saw as "getting the band back together." Ley and I already had the apartment, and now Paris had finally come down to join us. She was working for a large hotel chain, and her employers allowed her to transfer to their Dallas location. I began to see the Laws of Attraction at work. My enthusiasm for ABC was powerful enough to reassemble my team in another state for the purpose of doing something monumental. I was super-confident that we were about to take the world by storm.

Paris's job was in walking distance from our building. That meant there weren't really any transportation issues. Paris had always been athletic and in good shape, so she didn't really mind walking to work on her daily commutes. She said it gave her a chance to take in the beautiful scenery and to meet people. She did have the uncanny ability to meet and network on the spot. I made a mental note that I might need to get out and walk around Downtown Dallas more often.

Ley and I were both taking full-time classes toward our degrees. She was attending Maryland University through the military G.I. Bill, and I was attending Texas University. We were dedicated to making the proper investments into our future. Neither of us was working at the time and agreed that all of our spare time would be dedicated to ABC. It appeared that everyone was all in and ready to kick things into overdrive. I was no longer the only person, besides my dad, who saw the vision. It was time to get down to business. We started by buying food and a huge vision board. This was a technique that would help us all align ideas and actually visualize what the success of ABC might look like.

We started seriously mapping out our goals and courses of action. How to summarize our business model with a thirty-second "elevator pitch." Where to start pitching. Whom to pitch to. We even attended a couple of free business seminars here in Dallas. The effort was definitely there and the hungry instinct to be a force in the game kept me up late nights, working on my mission.

Quickly, we signed up our first school. The Board of Education was starving for any free service like ours—especially with the school budgets being far less than the prison budgets in most states. They were as eager to have us, as we were to be there. In my mind, this was like having already won the title and being written about in the history books. I was now doing what I saw "real philanthropists" doing when I was a student.

Unfortunately, things didn't go quite as well as my first experience, but they didn't go terribly, either. It all boiled down to experience. We could have put on a more polished presentation. Preparing for a larger audience entailed a lot more work than any of us anticipated. If nothing else, we learned that we needed to perfect the art of production before we started obligating ourselves to contracts. Businesswise, it was amateur night at the Apollo! Of course there was no money coming in. We hadn't figured out how to monetize the process yet. We were really just focused on getting our brand recognized. We all knew that we had something really special. The biggest problem was that I (well, my father and I) were the only ones spending money!

Needless to say, the girls lost interest quickly. It required a ton of time, effort, and money just for the reward of a job well done. Because of that, the project and the kids became less of a priority. To be honest, I got it. Here we were, three young women in our early twenties, trying to figure life out. It was difficult enough to survive with decent jobs and parental assistance. Add in the burden of trying to actually do something to help children, on a limited budget, and the typical social challenges—that was a delicate balancing act, to say the least. Not to mention, Ley, Paris, and I took time to travel the world (Colombia, Brazil, Paris, Jamaica, and Bermuda). We had also made a "Ride or Die" pact and gotten tattoos to commemorate the time in our lives when we had become "real" factors in the world.

2017 was supposed to be the "Year of the Diva" for us. (Beyoncé said a Diva is the female version of a hustler, right?)

In all honesty, it may have been too early to take on such a huge responsibility, let alone a humanitarian cause that was so massive. There is a reason that we typically only hear about the large, well-funded charitable organizations, such as March of Dimes, Salvation Army, the Bill and Melinda Gates Foundation, etc. "Nonprofit" work doesn't mean that they can operate without profits. Trust me; this is very much a business! Operating an NPO is probably even more difficult because a specified portion of the "profits" must be allocated for "charitable endeavors." Those clothes they sell at the Salvation Army have to help pay utilities and employees as well. Don't get it twisted!

In addition, this was my first real experience with business on this level. I was a whole corporation, from CEO to receptionist, without the office or the professional staff, let alone the income. I was essentially trying to turn lead into gold. Man, I was making so many mistakes. I really needed some help, but didn't realize which leak to plug first to stop the ship from sinking. Even choosing the right help turned out to be an experience in itself. I failed miserably at it. My first instinct was to turn to my family and friends. Some of them were less educated than I was and others were outright jealous and trying to sabotage us. That hurt.

My father always said, "Friends and family will drag you through the mud." What I didn't understand then, I truly understand now. When you partner with someone, they must be qualified to bring a specific skill set to the table, along with a work ethic that complements, matches, or exceeds yours. You must have strategic partners in order to succeed. One of my many faults is that I take people at face value, when I know in my heart (and from experience) that some are selfish, have ulterior motives, or are downright rotten to the core. I want to believe that people are inherently good, or at least as honestly ambitious as I am. It sounds silly to me now, because if integrity was so common, why would I put it so high on my resume?

I can hear my father saying, again: "Pooh, people have a strong propensity to follow their own desires and inclinations over your objectives and goals, so when dealing with them you gotta leave room for error and compensate by having a contingency plan in place." Words that I would someday have to learn to live by...or suffer heavily for ignoring.

***

LEY WAS THE first to bail out on ABC. Her lifestyle and nightlife activity were taking a toll on us all. We were trying to stay the course, and Ley was doing her thing! A perfect example: One morning, I was having a cup of coffee and doing some work at the dining room table when three people emerged from Ley's room, headed towards the front door. The guy was about six-foot-six, slender and muscular, and the girl was cute, with a stripper's body.

"Who is that?" the girl inquired about me.

"Oh, that's my sister. She's a square. She ain't into this type of shit," Ley told her as she gave them both a tongue kiss and slapped the girl on the ass.

"I had fun last night. Call me later," the man said, leaning in for another quick kiss.

I was shocked at what I was witnessing. Clearly, I was being punked, because this couldn't be happening right now, I told myself. I waited for everyone to turn around and yell, "Psych!" Instead, they were let out the door, and Ley turned around and headed back inside.

"What the fuck was that?" I asked her.

"I guess the cat is out the bag," she replied with a girly giggle. She then added, "Girl, I'm living my best life. Let me get a shower and let's go get something to eat."

She was so casual and matter-of-fact about the whole thing that I didn't know where to start or what to say. Not only did I feel slightly uncomfortable about the kind of people who were in our home, I was concerned about my girl. She was wilding out on a level that was foreign to the people we ran with. This girl was on some BET movie shit.

It turns out that ol' boy was a professional basketball player whom she'd known for years, and they had picked up ol' girl at a club. That information came courtesy of my facial expression. I guess she felt obligated to hip me to the new Ley and how she got down. The shocking part was that Ley was currently in a long-term relationship with a woman she'd met in the military. She told me they had been together for a couple of years. It occurred to me that she wasn't just a freak, but she was a cheater as well.

I was dying to know what happened to the sister whom I thought I knew everything about. I mean, I wasn't judging her...a lot. But I was thrown off and "perplexed" (that's a euphemism for what I really felt). She said that her "woman" was the first girl she ever slept with, but she was too jealous and controlling. She gave me a few other relationship details about how it first started and how she had always been curious. I listened and tried not to let my emotions play out on my face. This mess was blowing my mind!

How it got to the point of threesomes with random chicks, I didn't even want to know. It was like she was a lost soul, searching to fill a void. I actually felt sorry for her. I could hear the discontentment in what she didn't say: like, I'm happy, I feel complete, I've found my match...nothing close to that). There was no human connection or sense of honor in these acts, disguised as relationships. Just reckless, unadulterated promiscuous behavior.

When I told Paris, she didn't even pretend to be surprised. She had known for years and thought I knew too. I soon found out that everyone in our circle knew but me. Suddenly my main concern became how this had slipped past me. I had been schooled by the best. Why wasn't I able to peep this in her? Someone who I used to call my sister? We had shared all of our secrets and desires and even shared a bedroom. I felt green as hell.

The only thing that came to mind is what my father told me from jump..."*You don't know people until you've lived with them.*" And, "*After you've been separated for long periods of time, people have to be reevaluated, because people change.*" No one could have paid me to believe that anyone could change that much. What I was telling myself before, about feeling slightly uncomfortable about Ley's behavior, soon became a fear that something tragic would be the only outcome of her living this close to the edge. I just prayed that I was wrong.

Even with this new personality, we managed to renew our lease and keep the business end of the relationship working. We came into 2018 with separate agendas, but everyone stuck to the plan. No babies or marriages until we were prepared to succeed in life.

***

THIS BEHAVIOR WENT ON for a while. Ley was spending the night with different men and women. On some occasions, both. Finally I spoke up. I didn't care about her lifestyle. It was about respect. And though we had never laid down any rules, it was an unwritten rule that our place was a sanctuary. A place for peace and serenity. Neither Paris nor I had ever allowed a male guest to spend the night. I guess Ley didn't like the way the conversation went because one day, without any warning, she was gone. I had gone to Michigan to visit my father, and when I returned all her things were moved out.

I wasn't mad about her leaving. She deserved to live where she could be free to do what she wanted. However, we were in this together until the lease was up. So to say nothing when we still had six months left on a lease that we both signed for? That pissed me off! She'd left Paris and me holding the bag. I had no problem coming up with an additional $750 per month, but Paris's job didn't support that lifestyle, and she hadn't signed up for $2250 for rent. Soon Paris gave me her notice that she would be transferring back to Atlanta. I was sympathetic to her decision. It wasn't her fault that things had fallen apart.

I went to the leasing office to see if I could get out of the contract. That's when I found out that Ley had taken herself off the lease, and I was the sole lease holder. I discovered that while you're on military active duty, you can break any lease or rental agreement for deployment. She'd falsified some documents that said she was being deployed, and it was just that simple.

I drove over to Paris's place of employment to tell her what I had learned. I had only visited the building she worked in one other time, when Ley and I were apartment searching. This particular setup was a five-star hotel on one side and luxury apartments on the other. Paris had been a concierge manager for the company that owned it, before transferring to Dallas.

As I entered the lobby of the building, to my surprise, I saw Paris and Ley talking. From where I was standing, neither of them could see me. It had been nearly two full months since Ley had disappeared, but their conversation seemed friendly. My instinct was to run over there and punch her in the face, but my common sense kicked in quickly. Two things: One, I'd never punched anyone in the face before, let alone been in a fist fight. Two, it would have been even more embarrassing to get my ass kicked by a bitch who had served in the military. But trust me; I wasn't scared, just smarter than my anger. (Can you hear my dad talking about thinking through anger?)

Fuming, I just watched them chitchat. I wondered how Paris could be so cool after how our supposed "sister" had played us. A few minutes later, Ley walked over to the residential elevator and entered with a key card. Now it all made sense! I went home to do some thinking. My spidey sense was tingling, and I didn't ignore my intuition. Paris came home that night and we had a big blowup. It came out that she'd known the whole time, because she was the one who helped Ley get a discount in her building. I felt played and betrayed. My closest associates and people who had shared my home had conspired behind my back. That shit was hard to swallow, even with a keen understanding that people will typically place their agenda above the teams. (My dad's voice again.)

To make a long story short; Paris moved in with Ley. Now I was left holding the entire bag!

Believe me when I say that, "In the end, FAMILY is all we got." My dad agreed to pay the rent and car note for a couple of months until we came up with something. To break the lease would cost us the security deposit and a $10,000 fine. In my dad's mind, that was three months' rent that we would have to pay anyway. This was a sad time in my life. I felt like a failure. I had failed in my business ventures with my father and the girls, in my leadership, and financially. I was falling apart. It had quickly gone from the best of times to the worst of times. It almost felt like it couldn't get any worse.

***

WHILE I DIDN'T WANT to believe it, I had to consider that this was a play that Ley had laid down on me because of our past history. She had proven to me that she could be a cold and calculating person. Was this her revenge served cold? I wrestled with whether or not I truly believed that about us. Surely, she was cold, but we had grown up together and been sisters.

Then one day I went down to grab the mail. There were several letters to Ley from the bank and her attorneys. She must have forgotten to change her address or they made a mistake. Either way, all was fair in love and war. I opened and read each document. What I discovered came as no real surprise.

"...after further investigation and review of all the facts, we regret to inform you that our firm has decided that your claims have no merit. At this time, we must decline to take your case."

Wow, this bitch had been lying, scheming, and playing on people the whole time. How many others had she taken to that law office and had them wait in the lobby, besides me and ol' boy? Then there were several letters from the bank's loan officer. I recognized the name because he was our guy that Tee had hooked us up with.

Ley had doubled back and actually taken the 150k: personal loan, business loan, and line of credit for herself. How did Tee and I not find out about this? I wondered. In addition, she had cosigned for a 30k loan for her girlfriend in Maryland. The bank was informing her that all loan payments were in default.

What they didn't know was that she was long gone. I had to wonder how many more plays like this she had lain down. How many more of her people did she take to the bank? How did she get our guy to keep it a secret? Did she sleep with him too? Put one of her girls on him? Better yet, tag-team him? She was into that, apparently.

Damn, I'd never seen that coming! Where did she come up with this scandalous shit? She sure wasn't the innocent little girl I knew when we were growing up. But, I had to admit, I admired her gangsta. She was ruthless. Ley was 'bout that life! She was more than a shark, she was a pirate! I had to accept that I needed to sharpen my game, or instead of being at the table with hunters, I would be the one on the menu.

Chapter Eighteen:
Love & Betrayal

I T GOES WITHOUT SAYING that anyone who has ever trusted anyone has been disappointed at some point. That's a part of life that is inescapable. In fact, my dad warned me more times than I can count, and I heard his words again, like a broken record: "Pooh, people have a strong propensity to follow their own desires and inclinations over the objectives and goals of others, so when dealing with them you gotta leave room for error and compensate by having a contingency plan in place."

However, even a parent's sage advice could never prepare a child for certain levels of disappointment. In fact, the greatest setup is the expectation that there will be relationships built upon foundations of love and sacrifice that guarantee an unbreakable loyalty. Like a parent and child. Sisters and brothers. Lovers and friends. Well, maybe not your lovers or your friends.

We are led to believe that oaths and declarations before God are sacred. As naive as it may sound, I'd never expect someone to swear on their mother and be lying. In the Black community, that's enough of a violation of the culture to get you banned from the circle. As children, my dad and his "blood brothers" pricked their fingers with needles and mixed blood to seal their pact of loyalty. In my generation, my "sisters" and I got matching tattoos. We chose the Pac Man Ghosts to symbolize chasing paper. Each in different colors. Mine was the Red Ghost. Ley and Paris had them as well. We called it our Ride or Die Pact For Life. We vowed to always have each other's backs. The goal was to reach our full potential by waiting until we were successful enough to have children or get married, remain healthy, and chase our dreams.

While Ley already had tattoos, Paris and I did this as a leap of faith to prove our dedication to one another. The idea of having that needle permanently mark my body meant everything to me. I must have stared at my tattoo for two or three hours each day for more than a week. It was an ultimate sacrifice (and it hurt!). It may not even be possible, but for some reason, I felt even closer to the girls after we sealed our pact. It was as if we'd married our lives into one another's and there was no way that we could fail or that anyone could ever come between us.

Looking back on it, I suppose this is the same premise that fraternities and gangs are founded upon. A shared constitution. No room for error or need for a contingency plan. The solemn oath of "blood in, blood out." Till death. However, unlike others, ours was the real deal, right?

This stage of my life was a time of exploration and growth. I remember traveling to other countries and thinking that I knew more about the world than most women my age. It gave me a sense of wisdom and experience to be able to post pictures in Jamaica, Bermuda, and other places with my sisters. I was young, but I operated my own businesses, lived in a high-rise apartment with successful people, and didn't have the burden of reporting to a 9-to-5 each day. I attributed a large portion of my confidence to having a loyal support system and protective bubble. That sense of security is everything to a young woman embarking on making her place in the world.

Because I had recently ended my relationship with Jay, I was careful not to entertain anything too serious with any guy I dated. Jay and I remained friends, so I was able to still lean on him for aspects of my life that required a trustworthy male's perspective. That also made my newfound freedom to pursue greatness feel a little less daunting.

I wonder if it's just me, or have more women imagined that they could "lose" something and keep it at the same time? Like lose a lover and keep him as a friend? Even though it's very possible, have you ever asked yourself what that really looks like from another perspective? Like boundaries, or loyalty? Does he still sit on your bed when he comes over? Shower at your place and dry off with your towels? Eat what he wants from your refrigerator? Ask who gave you the flowers on the kitchen counter? Expect sex without protection? Kiss on the mouth? No, really? Doesn't a change of circumstances require that the rules be reestablished in terms of boundaries and expectations? Should the idea of loyalty remain unchanged, even when either of you becomes involved with someone new? Who gets priority in matters such as appropriate relationship conduct? If he always called you "Peaches," and your new man thinks it's inappropriate, where do you stand?

I know... I know... But if you share a bond with one, and a bed with another, shit gets complicated, so follow me. If you tell your ex to ignore five years of tradition and start calling you by your name for the sake of "new bae," what happens if you break up? Hmmm? Maybe you like the name and the comfort of a long-term friendship, although it makes others uncomfortable. More importantly, the ultimate reality is that an ex can't make you do anything to violate the new relationship that you didn't choose to do, right?

What if his new love interest is an adversary or enemy? The bitch who worked at his job and always flirted with him when you all were together? It gets deeper when the shoe is on the other foot, huh?

There are a million scenarios. Most are governed by a simple science that we like to call names like Girl Code, Guy Code, G-Code, etc. But it all boils down to respect for the boundaries of loyalty. Don't do the shit that an enemy would do to one another.

Point blank. I'm sure that when in doubt, most of us skip past the confusion and just go with whatever feels best, right? Too bad that life doesn't work like that for me. Rules and principles not only influence my decisions, but affect my conscience.

Trust and believe that the "less than loyal" friends of my exes have tried it. However, integrity precedes loyalty, and even when my loyalty isn't to the person, I'm always loyal to my principles.

If I thought that my actions would hurt a friend, I couldn't betray them by doing it and pretending that it didn't happen. I'm just not built to wear two faces with people I love or respect. He could be Prince Hakeem (The boy got his own money!) and he'd be forgotten yesterday. That means if you kissed him in the third grade, or even liked him and told me about it...exes are off limits! (Girl code 101.)

So having a new lover wouldn't allow me to disregard the respect owed to a former "love." Not everyone feels that way, but in this new age of selfishness and cutthroat savagery, I'm extra careful to be conscious of boundaries. If I no longer considered someone worthy of respect and loyalty, I'd just end all association.

***

DESPITE WHAT MY DAD taught me, I never imagined that I'd one day live in a time when betrayal is the new loyalty. Mediocrity is the new excellence. And lies are the new truth. People who live with integrity are the minority. So, much like my coveted purse collection, exclusive editions are in much higher demand. I'd much rather be one of the few than one of the many. The worst version of reality is when supposed friends/family members conspire to betray you. The idea that either could have/should have said "This is wrong," but neither did, is mind-blowing. For most of us, that is the hardest pill to swallow. Yet, all over the world, people are disregarding the basic principles of respect in search of self-satisfaction.

I've been warned: "Never allow a female friend to move in with you and your man. The boundaries get crossed and eventually inappropriate things happen."

Thus, I never put myself in that position. That doesn't guarantee that people won't go out of their way to violate your trust, but at least you don't invite them to. If you're wondering why I took the time to address this subject, I think the answer is obvious: I've suffered from the scars of betrayal and learned a lesson that helped to build my character!

I have accepted that the world I live in will not always treat me fairly. That being the victim of another's lack of principle doesn't make me the biggest loser in the situation. Of course it reinforced the harsh reality that my parents attempted to teach me, but it didn't kill me or stop my flow.

A friend of mine likes to say, "You can never be betrayed by a stranger."

His philosophy is, "It requires that you actually trust someone for them to betray you. However, to never trust anyone is to have been betrayed 1,000 times, without actually having ever experienced the beauty of loyalty."

I agree wholeheartedly. That's the greater of two evils. Thus, I have forgiven the unforgivable sins of false love or selfish agendas. Why? Because I would never return the favor of betrayal. Not because I would suffer the agony of never trusting again. That would be the definition of defeat. Emotional paralysis. To be sentenced to a life of cowardice and missed opportunities because of someone else's crimes against integrity? I think not!

So at times we experience the worst pain, not from the wounds of enemies, but the cyanide-laced kisses of friends. Maybe those episodes were merely lapses in judgement? Given a chance, they would rewrite the history? Perhaps their good deeds outweigh the bad? Those are factors to be considered by the injured party.

However, the better assessment of the circumstances requires more logic than emotion. You have to ask yourself, what rationale justifies trusting someone who PLOTTED to deceive and violate the basic principles of trust from the start? Unless you simply trust them to be who they are...

Chapter Nineteen:
Making Mistakes "Growing Pains"

P LEASE KEEP IN MIND that it is difficult for me to talk about this period in my life. My father insisted that I talk about this phase because these difficult lessons helped me become a woman, a better person, and drew him and me closer.

***

LOOKING BACK ON SOME of the mistakes I made, it seems it didn't come as a surprise to my father that I would fail in that moment. (I have mentioned this before, but it's an important parenting lesson that I hope many will heed.) When I got older and asked why he wasn't as disappointed as I thought he would be, his answer was simple: "I failed the first time I did it that way."

He allowed me to make some mistakes (at his expense), knowing that learning those invaluable lessons firsthand would only strengthen me for my journey. Of course, other times when I made a mistake, he didn't spare bruising my little ego. I'd be trying to justify my actions and he'd say something like: "That's the dumbest s@#t I ever heard in my life! What in the hell were you thinking about?"

My dad hates excuses with a passion. He calls it "deceptive intelligence"—he finds the idea that you would put extra energy into supporting a false narrative as opposed to fixing the issue unforgivable. If you own it, we can move on. I'm like him in this respect.

If you keep trying to convince me of the logic in your unreasonable thinking, you're either lying, laying down a play on me (being deceptive), or delusional. None of these can be good for the relationship, and we'll never have a fruitful association if you think that what you've done is okay to do again. The other thing my dad hates—from me and only me—is sarcasm and when I talk back. He views it as disrespect. He's often said, "You think I won't smack your little ass in the mouth through this phone?"

I'm thinking, *How the hell are you gonna do that?* He certainly made it sound as if it were possible to do. I learned later in life that he didn't mean "physically" slap me. He had other methods to inflict pain that would last much longer than a physical slap. If he stepped on me (told me about myself with no filter), that would have been the equivalent of a slap. We didn't step on each other, but I'd seen him step on others with no mercy! When others were sarcastic, he just shut them down with more wit and sarcasm in return. It was like an intellectual challenge or mental gymnastics for him. The goal was to force the lesser opponent to concede. If they got angry, he knew he had them and moved in for the kill. (Again...his motto is: "Think through anger!")

If the mistake was really damaging, he'd say: "We're in damage control. Let's fix the problem first, then we'll come back to the lesson, so it won't happen again."

No, he's not going to skip the lesson. He really wants you to explain the thinking process that you went through to come up with such a dumbass idea!

Now I understand there was a method to his madness. Going back through the process allowed you to discover the flaws in your thinking and highlight what (or what not) to do in the future, in order to succeed. When things get serious, you can't afford to panic. You have to go into thinking mode...and fast.

My dad didn't have time to fuss when he was assessing the damage and trying to find the right solution in a given moment. He understood that the learning process entails making mistakes. The objective is to reduce the adverse effects. Having to do damage control is far more costly than doing damage prevention. And as my father would say: "Your next move has to be your best move, but also the winning move!" There is a huge difference.

***

WHEN I WAS GROWING up, my father didn't curse me out much, but he certainly "fussed" me out at times (to put it mildly). I often wondered whether, if he'd been at home, he'd have been the kind of parent who spared the rod, or the kind who whooped ass. Knowing my father, his motives and objectives are always motivated by helping us to learn lessons that would help us in life. So I would like to think that he would have been strategic, because that's how he moves now.

If he had applied the latter, both of my knucklehead brothers would be dead! Speaking of dumb, knuckleheaded moves...I was certainly glad that he wasn't home when I messed up his money! After all, we were talking about my father, and the man's reputation preceded him. I was his daughter, so I wasn't worried about any physical harm. Plus, he wasn't a violent man anymore. He had this religious peace thing going on in his life. He was in a good place, mentally, physically, and spiritually...I hoped.

Yet, I was worried about the disruption, chaos, and damage I'd caused between us. I had witnessed him cut people off, even relatives, for less. (That's how I became his Chief Financial Officer!)

After I came to my senses, the thought of our relationship being irreparably broken drove me into an even deeper depression. It's crazy how everybody, except for my mother, thought I was tripping because I was broke. She understood exactly what it was. It wasn't ideal, but I could live without money. I wasn't that shallow. She knew, just like I did, that I was my father's daughter. There would be other opportunities to get some money, and I would certainly find a way. However, it would be difficult to live with the fact that I had destroyed the relationship with my dad, or accept that our relationship would never be the same because of something I'd done. The idea that I had become one of those people on his list of undesirable associations was too much to digest, and it scared me to death! I wasn't like them. I just had to prove it.

If you know my father, then you know he's 'bout his paper! That's one thing that he doesn't play about. As I mentioned earlier, in my early twenties, I started handling his money and important affairs. Things started off smoothly, and I must have passed all his mental agility tests, because he started trusting me with more money and responsibilities.

I had already experienced some business failures of my own, worked a couple of jobs, and decided that I didn't want to work for anybody. So his tutelage was everything to me. At the time, I was struggling from one hustle to another. My "so-called" hustle partner, Ley, had left me holding the bag with rent and bills, and I was desperate to find a solution. Even with my father stepping up to pay the rent and car note for three months, I still had to cover the insurance and other bills. What he didn't know was that I was already a month behind on rent and three months behind on car payments.

Being the genius that I was, I still tried to finesse his solution by catching up on bills and using the rest of the allotted money to hustle with. Long before sites like Poshmark, Mercari, or such avenues existed, I had started an online boutique. I maintained a few high-end clients whom I supplied with new and used handbags. My business model was simple. I would buy bags from anyone who needed cash and resell them. When a client requested a specific type of new or used bag, I would procure it for them. All online, no overhead. With a small markup, I was making a few dollars, but nothing to write home about.

A few months later, my dad finally came up with a plan. To say that I didn't like it would be an understatement! He suggested that when my lease was up, I move back in with my mother for a few months, in order to regroup.

I was like, "What!"

He also told me to sell my car because I was in what is called an "upside-down loan." He told me that he would buy me a "cash car" (basic reliable transportation). But wait...on top of that; he said I should sell my bags to accumulate some operating cash. I had collected a beautiful array of handbags that I was proud of. I had been infatuated with purses since I was a toddler. On top of it all, he suggested that I get a JOB! The tradeoff was that I could keep my clothes and jewelry. He had to be losing his mind.

I was thinking, *why create this ambitious animal if you planned to keep me in a cage?*

I was livid, to say the least. Not only was I dead broke, but he wanted me to sell all my possessions and go live with my mother! Lauren Washington couldn't go from penthouse suite to mama's couch. BMW to a Chevy Malibu. Sell my bags and jewelry and get a job. Hell no!

Don't even think, "Sell my possessions."

The better plan was, he could just loan me the money until I got something going. His answer made me mad as hell. He had the nerve to tell me, "I don't feel comfortable loaning you anything. You don't have the means to pay me back."

Oh, really? Now that I'm down, you're going to kick me? Of course I didn't actually intend to pay him back, but he was my father; I felt like he could just bail me out and give me a fresh start. That's what he was there for, right?

Wrong answer!

However, he did give me one of his lectures, for free. "Pooh, I don't live in a penthouse, drive a BMW, or carry my phone in a ten-thousand-dollar bag." He told me that I didn't need those things, and I should have listened to him.

I really hated when he told me, "You're too busy trying to look rich, instead of trying to get rich."

I don't know why I was under the illusion that he didn't know what it was like out here and I needed nice things to be taken seriously.

Just for the record, anyone who doesn't know what to do if you find yourself in this predicament: downgrade until you get your chips back up. You don't keep throwing good money at bad situations. Part of having a keen sense of business is knowing when to cut your losses. Most beginners don't realize that every hustler goes through this phase. No matter what level you're on, struggling is a part of life. Things not going according to plan is also a part of life. There's no shame at failing at a venture, as long as you gain valuable lessons from the experience.

Because I was inexperienced in this aspect of the game, I was trying to hold onto everything I had accumulated. I didn't understand that savvy hustlers made those big purchases, not just to look good, but as investments for when things called for extra capital. With collateral, you could cut your losses, liquidate, get some cash, and get back on your feet. That's why cars, clothing, and cheap jewelry are a poor investment. All of those things decrease in value immediately after the purchase. That's Business 101.

At the time, I didn't know that what my father was trying to teach me was financial security and independence. I didn't understand what he meant by, "I'd rather have enough money in the bank to purchase everything I want, than to simply have everything I want."

Now, it's obvious. We typically want more than what we need or can afford.

***

YET, I STILL RENEWED my lease, while refusing to decrease my spending habits. I was primarily focused on trying to maintain the lavish lifestyle I had become accustomed to. I was afraid to lose all the material possessions that I thought made me the woman I was. In my mind, it would be even more embarrassing to look broke, in addition to having no money. I had to make something happen and quick!

I was making one bad financial decision after another. Everyone close to me was trying to warn me that my life was spiraling out of control. To be honest, I remember questioning myself as to what I'd done to get there. According to the blueprint for success, I had done it all right up until that point. I didn't use drugs. I hadn't gotten pregnant. I'd finished my undergraduate degree. Didn't that automatically validate that I deserved to spoil myself with the finer things in life? That's what I told myself, at least. What I forgot to calculate was the amount of hard work it took to afford that nice life.

"Too busy trying to look rich…instead of trying to get rich."

Now I understood what my father meant by, "What common people see is the end result of a production. They never consider all the details of the hard work, or blood, sweat, and tears that goes into making something a success."

He would always say: "If you wanna be great, you gotta do all the extraordinary things that great people do. When everyone else is playing, you gotta be putting in work. When everyone else is on vacation, you gotta be putting in work. When everyone else is sleeping, you gotta be up putting in work."

It became apparent that my failure at this point was my own doing. I hadn't been putting in enough work. The time I spent making power moves was overshadowed by the profits I spent making foolish investments; and having fun small victories made me lose track of the larger goal. Wealth!

"Every milestone must be acknowledged, but never celebrated if you want more. Do you think a championship team celebrates its first win in an eighty-two-game season?" he'd say.

In retrospect, I realize that running into complications in my personal life caused me to get sidetracked and forget one of my dad's cardinal rules: "Lean on your strengths, and learn to manage your weaknesses."

I thought about all the lessons I had been taught and how I had failed to apply them. I could hear his voice in my head right then: "You can have all the knowledge in the world, but it's useless if you can't put it into practicality. Apply it so that it benefits you."

Man, how would we learn all of this without the pains of the experiences? Is it even possible? The saying that "Experience is the best teacher" is one of the most expensive lessons to learn. In fact, it has cost some of us a price that we can never afford to pay. If we could bottle the whole process and make it less painful, we'd be rich for sure!

***

I MADE ONE BAD choice after another. I was delusional about my financial situation, and having access to my father's credit card and cash in the bank didn't make it any better. I told myself that I was smart. Not just some slick chick with a hustle hand. I actually had a degree and managed to live, dress, and drive alongside the best of them. I'd done it without corporate America and their biweekly slave wages. I felt entitled. After all, I helped my dad get to the position he was in by managing his affairs, right? We were partners. I figured that what was his was also mine.

Wrong answer again!

That was the attitude of a spoiled brat and a sign of immaturity. No one is ever entitled to anything that belongs to somebody else. No matter how close you are. No matter how long you've worked together or what type of work you put in. Do you think a person who has managed a Walmart store for thirty years can just take 100k out of a company account because he fell on hard times? If you do, your ass is going to prison. It's called stealing; embezzlement, fraud...and you'd better not do it to a gangster! According to the street law, that's a one-way trip to the grave.

Needless to say, my lifestyle, financial woes, arrogance, ignorance, and inability to listen caused a rift in my relationship with my father. This immature attitude caused me to make the biggest mistake of my life. I felt like I didn't need him if he wasn't going to help me. I could figure it out on my own. I had the skills, the knowledge, and his money. (I swear, the term "temporary insanity" is a real thing!)

I tried to reason that what I was doing was best for us. I don't know if I was looking for a reason to undermine his position because I had access to his money, or if I felt like I deserved it because he wasn't there for me as a child. Or was it because he was refusing to help me in the way that I decided I needed help? It occurred to me that maybe I was trying to be bolder and more vicious, like Ley, because of the move that she had laid down on me. Maybe it was a combination of it all. I guess I needed to be mad at him in order to violate his trust. I needed someone to blame for my acts of betrayal. As if it wouldn't be so low of me, if I conjured up some reason why.

This was all the sum of my immaturity and justified bullshit. This man had been there for me all my life. He'd given me everything that I ever asked for and more—from prison! He had been more of a father to me than any of my friends or family members could say their fathers in the free world had. I had simply ignored my impeccable breeding and gone against everything in me to be a disloyal thief, and I was ashamed of myself.

At some point, we must accept that the bad decisions we make are our own. We sometimes put our agendas above the principles of respect and integrity. I did that to my own father. What kind of human was I? This was one of those times in life when my actions hurt me more than anyone else. I still suffer while writing this. No sin against family is worse than betrayal.

***

THE YEARS 2018 into 2019 were a bad time in my life. My dad did everything in his power to help me out, without spoiling me further. He understood that I needed to learn some hard lessons in life, in order to prepare me for my journey into independence. Plus, he had a thing against making a poor hustler out of me.

In real time, however, due to the combination of my arrogance and lack of experience, I never truly understood or listened to what anyone was telling me unless they had an immediate fix for my problem. My life was spiraling out of control, and I needed to be spoiled with a bailout. Not to be taught a lesson in life! A foreign concept to my dad.

It's strange that all the things I deem insignificant now were major back then. I was in a bad place physically, mentally, and spiritually. It's difficult to focus when you're in an unhealthy state of mind. I'd become accustomed to a luxurious lifestyle, and everything was threatening to fall apart. At this time, I was practically back at home with Mama and my sister Maddy. I was spending way more time with them than I was at my "soon-to-be evicted-from" apartment downtown. My existence on Earth consisted of one problem: I needed money and I needed it fast!

And just when I was convinced that things couldn't get any worse, my car got repossessed. After being unable to make the payments, it never occurred to me that I was using my mother's address to finance the damn car! While I figured that I was hiding out, I was right where they were looking. They must have sent Pookie and Ray Ray, I guess, because they definitely came and got their BMW. Hell, I didn't need a car anyway. I didn't have anywhere to go!

After losing my BMW, I was now renting a luxury car. Another bad business decision, but a girl has a reputation to uphold, right? I should have leased a car under one of our businesses, or bought a cash car to get around, like my dad advised.

Thank God that I was smart enough to not to mess up our business credit! That would prove to be an invaluable business decision later on. I've since realized that in business and personal matters, you can never afford to be overly emotionally attached. Sometimes you have to assess a situation and make the hard decision of folding, no matter how much time, money, or resources you have invested. Chalk up your losses; take it on the chin, and move on to the next gig.

My father calls it "the Exit Strategy"—a tactic he wishes he'd developed in his hustling days. His current business philosophy was that you had to go into every business endeavor with an exit strategy because nothing lasts forever. He said that when they were young, my mother used to warn him of that constantly. Good sense dictates that you never continue to throw good money, time, and energy at a bad situation; and certainly, never go down with a sinking ship. Especially when the world is offering a thousand lifeboats to carry you to safety.

It seems another bad (good) quality I hadn't yet learned to manage back then was the fact that I'm not a quitter. Quitting while you're ahead isn't the same thing as quitting. I had the vain perception that you did not accept a plan had failed until there was just no hope left. That was the equivalent of being beaten to death, instead of running away to recover and returning with a vengeance.

I guess I learned the hard way that "A hard head makes a soft behind."

If you refuse to take good advice, you'd better get used to falling on your butt!

***

ONE MORNING I HAD just finished working out when I ran into this man on the elevator in my building. I knew that he lived in the penthouse. He looked to only be a few years older than I was at the time (late twenties, early thirties). He was tall, slender, and wore cheap suits, but he didn't wear cheap cologne. He always smelled good.

He was a cute white guy who had this Brad Pitt look going. He personified something that I noticed about wealthy white people: you could never gauge their income by their attire. While most of us poorer people spent a great deal of our money "looking good and playing rich," white folk often dressed down and concealed their wealth behind real estate, investments, and stocks.

We'd occasionally bumped into one another previously, but this time we actually conversed.

"Hey, I've seen you before. You're one of those fine women who live on the seventeenth floor, right?"

"And you're the rich white guy who lives in the penthouse on the top floor, right?" I replied sarcastically, letting him know that I knew who he was and where he lived as well.

"Oh, I didn't mean to come off like a stalker," he assured me, sensing my discomfort with his knowing my apartment location. "To answer your question, I don't actually stay in the penthouse. I use it for passive income. I have a far less expensive single unit on the other side of the building."

Now he had my attention. "What do you mean by passive income?" I inquired.

"Have you ever heard of AirBnB?"

I confirmed that I had.

"Well, I pay a monthly fee to use that platform to list my unit."

"How much do you rent the unit for?" I asked with my antennas up.

"On the high end, $1,400 per night, and $1,000 on the low. I usually book about twenty days out of a month."

"What?" I said as the lightbulb and calculator went off in my head. *Damn, that's 20k per month on the low end,* I calculated quickly.

"Whenever you see me on this side, I'm usually doing a walk-through after a client has left," he informed me as the elevator stopped on my floor. Being a gentleman, he held the door open for me and asked what I did for a living.

"I run a nonprofit for anti-bullying," I replied, ashamed of the whole truth. ABC was the only good thing I still had going on.

"Why don't you tell me about it over a cup of coffee if you have the time?" he suggested professionally, sounding really interested.

"I have a meeting at Starbucks. Why don't you pull up in about an hour?"

Like many of my entrepreneurial counterparts, Starbucks often served as a makeshift office where I enjoyed free WiFi and a safe public space. With all the weirdos running around, a woman can never be too careful.

"Pull up?" he asked, as if the lingo was foreign to him. "Oh yeah, yeah, I'll absolutely pull up on you," he said after catching on.

"All right, I'll see you then."

I excused myself to prepare for whatever might come of this encounter. What I understood about younger people was that no matter the ethnicity, everyone was intrigued by Black culture. A whole generation wanted to be hip and in the loop. Especially young, white, entrepreneurs.

I ran to my computer, Googled AirBnB, read enough to familiarize myself with the company, and then called Tee. "Google AirBnB and meet me at MY Starbucks in forty-five minutes. I got somebody I want you to meet."

"MY Starbucks" was code for the location near me and YOUR Starbucks was code for the one near her.

As soon as I jumped into the shower, I began thinking about two things: the questions I would ask, and the ones he would have for me. I didn't waste opportunities, and this felt like one of those times where I might just learn something that took me and my ambitions to the next level.

Less than an hour later, Tee and I were in Starbucks, looking like two of America's Next Top Models and CEOs. After the formal introductions, it was time to get down to business. Tee and I were on him like a couple of hungry hyenas. We needed this game, and he was more than willing to share. He even walked us through setting up a profile, invited us to take a look at his unit, and even encouraged us to tip the concierge manager. He informed us that in return, they would keep our business on the low and service our clients. Apparently, in all business endeavors, cheddar made it better. Greasing palms was just another intelligent tactic used by those who understood profit-sharing as a way of earning favor. He gave us a few more tricks of the trade, and we were off and running.

The beautiful thing about the AirBnB platform was that you set your own rates and you could change them at any time. I just so happened to have a high-rise apartment on the seventeenth floor, with three bedrooms and three baths, in Downtown Dallas. That was a great product to begin with. It cost me over four grand a month to throw that address around. Aside from that, everything was in walking distance. I felt confident that people would want to rent my unit, if I could give them a competitive price. Talk about perfect timing! I had visions of going from poverty to the penthouse in one move. I set my prime rate at $600 per night. My hope was that I could rent my apartment for between seven and ten days per month. I calculated that $6,000 would cover the bills and give me some wiggle room.

To my surprise, I got three bookings in the first hour of posting the unit. Within a week, we were booked for the entire month. People were booking multiple days and even whole weeks. In the first month, I booked a total of twenty-seven out of thirty days. Seventeen of those days were at the full $600 rate, and the other ten days were discounted at around $475 per night. Totaling $14,950.

The trick was to lower the rate when you approach unbooked days. For example, if Wednesday was unbooked by Monday, I would give a discounted rate of $550. Tuesday $450, if I had to. Before the 2pm check-in on Wednesday, I'd even go as low as $200.

I considered that even if I only made a hundred dollars a day, at least I made something. During this time, something was better than nothing at all. That first month, making close to 15k set my hustler's mind ablaze. Because this business was so lucrative and fast-paced, I needed to find a way to scale...right now!

I used the majority of the money to get caught up on the rent, pay some bills, and stack a few chips. This was the type of thing I knew my dad would be proud of (or so I thought).

He was proud of me for finding a quick solution to my cash flow problem, but it didn't come without his complete and thorough assessment of the whole situation. I always seemed to overlook the fact that he was the kind of man to consider the possible flaws in any plan. He gave me a checklist, some instructions, and other things to consider. The first of which was a question that should have been foremost in my mind: whether I was gambling with doing it, or not.

"Pooh, are you sure that you're allowed to sublet?" came the first question.

He also said that I needed to add "no fault" liability to my renters insurance. He advised me not to rent to young people. It was safer to rent to families and professionals. I needed to create a contract that prohibited parties or more than seven guests. Add a contractual clause that assessed any breach of the agreement a $10,000 penalty. The list went on. The last of which he added, "Get your carrier's permit."

I'm like, "Dad, you're trippin."

Why go through all that? We were already listed and getting money. We were booked out for the next three months at our prime rate, and using my pricing system, I was sure that I could book the entire year. I was in a win-win situation, and he was worried about the wrong things, I thought to myself.

I don't know why I was under the impression that this was a new business concept and that he could learn something from me finally. This was one time in my life when my dad didn't know everything about the hustle, and I would show him that I had us. The fact was that there wasn't anything new about Bed and Breakfast (thus, BnB) home-slash-hotelier businesses, except that it had been repackaged into a viable online platform, where a parent company received a fee for listing your particular unit to the public. Clever. Not rocket science.

I had to be a fool to think that my dad didn't understand the commercial concept, when he and my uncles had amassed a total of twenty-one rental properties before he went to prison. For years, he had taken care of us, using the income from those properties. Despite his proven track record, I had the new game working for me and I considered my newfound success to be proof of the slogan, "Work smarter and not harder." My dad and the world was being put on notice, Lauren Washington was back!

***

THERE IS A SAYING that goes: "A fool knows everything but their own foolishness." Once again, I should have listened, but you know me...I blew it off. The money that was coming in was too good to change anything. The second and third months were as good as the first and proved that my business model was working. I was making a minimum of 15k per month, 9k profit. I couldn't believe it! That gave me the false sense of confidence that now was the time to reclaim my lost throne. It was time to get myself a new car, find a new (albeit less expensive) apartment, and get back on my feet. I didn't need a lavish penthouse (yet). I planned to rent a single-bedroom apartment and play it like the white dude had.

With all my intelligence, I made sense out of such an amateur move. Three months wasn't remotely enough time to factor in all the data of what could go wrong with a new business endeavor. Could you imagine if GM based their entire year on first quarter earnings alone? Never mind factoring in seasonal behaviors of consumers or economic changes.

I heard my dad's voice in my head: "Stay with your mom for about a year and stack your chips."

That was easy for him to say. While I was grateful for supportive parents, back then, I needed my own personal space. (You can imagine why.)

At this point, I was still in my luxury rental car. Bad move #1. The better move would have been a cash car to get me from point A to point B. I soon moved into a one-bedroom apartment with a six-month lease, that I could barely afford. Bad Move #2. That added stress to what could have been a stress-free arrangement with my mom. It was a downgrade from the deluxe apartment in the sky, but an upgrade from mama's couch, so I justified it.

Now I really needed to stack some chips, but every dollar made was allocated to something already. I ended up burning through my dad's cash faster than I anticipated. So it became more about just putting his money back than saving up money of my own. There was no telling when he might need the money, and not having it on hand was a major source of anxiety for me.

I managed to cut back on my spending and began budgeting to acquire only the absolute necessities. The crazy thing is that I was still spending more time at my mother's place than my own. However, I relished the convenience of going home when I wanted, or needed some space to get my head together. It probably would've been cheaper to live with my mom and rent an AirBNB once in a while, huh?

***

MEANWHILE, MY SECONDARY HUSTLE, an online boutique called Lolatee, was picking up as well. I sold high-end designer bags that were hard to find without traveling out of state, and in some cases, out of the country. It was fortunate for me that I happened to have a great connection. I had a client Tee had turned me on to some time ago. He requested two large Birkin bags, Togo Crevette 35s. They retail for $12,995 each. I could get them for 8k each through my connect and resell for $11,000, out the door!

I was happy to have the order, but I kept thinking, "The nerve of men!" The client had no problem telling me that one Birkin was for his wife and the other for his mistress. Not only did these women share a man (likely unknowingly), but they would also be sporting the exact same bag...in the same color.

As a woman, I ascribe to the belief that we share a collective responsibility to never support this type of behavior. Some of us call it "Girl Code." (That's a topic for a whole other book!) However, I was hustling for my life. I couldn't allow the feelings that govern my own personal constitution to interfere with my business. I stood to make six bands off of that transaction. Nothing to sneeze at.

And what did I know? He may have had an understanding with these women. In addition, if he didn't buy the bags from me, he would have bought them from someone else. Plus, that was bill money, and Lord knows I had bills to pay. (Was that too many excuses for supporting that man's bullshit in the name of profit? Okay, guilty as charged!)

Anyway, he sent the customary 20% nonrefundable deposit of $4,400, and I put that with $11,600 of my personal cash and purchased the bags. I was holding them, awaiting his funds to arrive to finalize the transaction. He had always been punctual in the past and spent good money with me, so I assumed this was a done deal. Even after a few days of no communication, I saw no reason to be alarmed.

***

EVERYTHING SEEMED TO BE going perfectly. One of my AirBnB clients was the Chief Marketing Executive of Nike. Knowing that cross-promoting is very important in branding, I would always leave an ABC and Lolatee gift bag for each client. The Nike exec was so intrigued by our cause that she wanted to discuss over lunch how she could help. The client was a very beautiful Black woman in her late forties. She looked fifteen years younger, and you could tell from her posture that she worked out. She also exuded the confidence of a woman who knew her stuff.

After the lunch meeting, I was convinced that she was the real deal. Later that same afternoon, I received a call from Nike's HR Corporate Community Give Back division, and just like that, Nike sponsored five seminars for underprivileged urban schools.

This unexpected stroke of good fortune forced me to quickly put together a team of professionals. Kiesha and my girl Lexis came through as always. Michigan State Representative Jewell Jones came onboard and introduced us to one of the most dynamic motivational speakers I've heard to this day: Shawn T. Blanchard. These young Black men were well respected in their fields, educated, and the youth were receptive to their delivery. We would open the events, and Jewell and Shawn closed them. I learned a lot about professionalism by working with them. Those events turned out to be the start of something big!

In addition, our Nike executive was so impressed with our unit's accommodations that she referred another client to us, one of her colleagues. The colleague was coming to Dallas for a job transfer and wanted to lease a corporate apartment for a year. That was an ideal situation for me. We agreed to 9k per month. That was half of what I could make by slow-rolling my daily bookings, but a safer bet.

DBR 101: "The fast flip is the way to get your money up fast."

Or, as J.C. says, "A fast nickel beats a slow dime every time."

The operational costs of daily living often work against the potential of a slow roll. By the time you pay into the routine costs from a slow roll, you haven't accumulated enough surplus cash to invest when an opportunity arises. Squeezing the highest profits from a product is an outdated business model in the days of Amazon's and Walmart's "price match."

The ideal business has a lower profit margin, with a more consistent volume. With the apartment cost of four grand per month, I would earn 5k on the rental at 9k, which totaled 60k per year guaranteed. The new client was ready for me to send over the contract for her attorney to review, and upon approval, her company would cut me a check for the first and last month's rent, plus security deposit. This was a hustler's dream: A self-contained, profitable, turnkey entity.

Once I secured this deal, signed, sealed and delivered, I would have the cushion to move on to the next venture. You know that my mind was turning with the realization that a lot more people would pay good money to experience the high-end amenities and ambience of our unit and the building. It was like experiencing the luxury living of a residence, with all the amenities of a ritzy hotel. Those were two of the very reasons I lived downtown. I began dreaming of ways to secure ten more high-end units.

***

IT'S ALWAYS A GOOD feeling when everything is going according to plan. However, becoming comfortable is forgetting that adversity awaits around every corner, looking for an opportunity to strike. After what I had just gone through, I didn't plan to ever be broke again!

I began to be able to stack a few chips on the side and made the critical decision to use more of my father's money to lease two more apartments. That would triple our income and show him that I was back on top of my game. Surely, I would finally get the accolades and praise that I deserved after bouncing back from near disaster, right?

With a little research, I found a new luxury high-rise offering two month's free rent with a one-year lease. With these high-end luxury living arrangements, there's always a gimmick. The application fee was a nonrefundable $600, and the free rent was cleverly prorated. You still had to drop the first and last month's rent. Thus, they still got their money monthly.

It was more apparent than ever that everybody was in on the hustle. The only thing I was mad about was that I was on the wrong end!

I knew my credit score wouldn't allow me to get the apartments, so I did a corporate lease. My real estate investment company was relatively new, so they wanted a corporate office guarantor. Too easy. My mother was one of the partners and had a good credit score.

She was more than willing to sign the lease. She was thoroughly invested in seeing me succeed, and I reciprocated by paying her $500 per month for the use of her services.

One of the apartments was a luxurious 2800 sq. ft. three-bedroom, four-bath penthouse suite. Rent was $6,200. The prorated discount would reduce it to $5,167. The second apartment was a two-bedroom, two-bath 1,800 sq. ft. on the eighth floor. The rent was $4,400, discounted to $3,667. With another $2,200 in miscellaneous bills and expenses ($500 for concierge, $500 for guarantor, and $1,200 in bills), we were looking at roughly $11,000 a month for this location.

I could book the penthouse for $1,500 on the high end and $1,000 on the low. The other unit would be $600 per night. We made reference to the apartments by number: one, two, and the penthouse being three. Now the only problem we had was to furnish these luxury units with items that would complement the asking price. High-end AirBnB units were expected to provide the customer with an ambience and decor that you didn't get in a typical hotel suite. This guaranteed a higher level of comfort along with the security of a private home.

I found a staging company that provided furnishing for whatever budget you had in mind. I made one-time purchases for the smaller items and rented the larger items, like the grand piano, Italian sofas,

60-inch televisions, and washer and dryer units. This added to our overhead, but we needed furnishings. We were selling class.

The furnishings arrived, we listed the units, and in no time, the bookings started coming in. I would only need to book each unit for an average of seven nights a month, at our prime rate, to cover the bills. Everything else would be gross that went towards breaking even on the initial investment. If these additional locations did as well as our first one, we'd be netting profit in no time at all.

***

ONE OF MY DAD'S infamous sayings is: "Never make exceptions to the rules. When you do, you leave room for errors." Our individual paradigms shape us into the people we become. Through our experience, we develop rules that govern how we deal with people. In the natural process of growth, we cultivate these factors and learn what works best for us. If you are good, you form a skill set that puts you in a winning position at every juncture. In some cases, that entails compromise. In other cases, complete rejection of certain things. At other times, avoidance.

The most important thing is to acquire the ability to identify and apply what works for you. When you do, never go outside the scope of your knowledge without seriously assessing all other possible outcomes. This was an adroit insight that helped me in every aspect of my personal and business affairs. Thus, I'm a creature of habit. Surely, I wasn't lacking the harsh life experiences. I paid for them in full. However, I never complain for two reasons: One, I never heard my father complain about his life. Here is a man who had it all. He was smart, handsome, ghetto rich, a hood legend, and a local celebrity. As his fate and the harsh realities of our life would have it, he now faces the possibility of death in prison for his improprieties, indiscretions, and bad decisions. In a recent letter to the parole board, he said many powerful things, but there's one I want to share, because it pertains to us all. He writes, "While I am not proud of the actions that set me on this course, I'm proud of the man I've become. I could not have become who I am without the journey. "

If my father refuses to complain about his position in life, who am I, or who are we, to complain? That's probably why we both detest whiners and complainers. To contextualize his statement, I apply it to myself in realization that I could not have become the woman I am today without my journey. The good and the bad of it.

What I've learned over the years is that the peaks and valleys of life are equally necessary to shape our perspectives. There is no way to escape the consequences of our bad decisions. Our lives will unfailingly reflect the choices we make. In some form or fashion, actions always catch up to us. Challenges are a part of life. After solving any current problem, another is sure to arise. To attempt to avoid having problems in life is an exercise in futility. The key is to avoid what you can, and minimize the damage from what you can't by developing effective problem-solving skills. A little luck helps, but as the old saying goes, "The man who was lucky his whole life probably didn't live very long."

Or, as my father would say: "Have you ever noticed that the people who have been through the most shit always have the most answers?"

It's apparent that you can't sharpen your skills enough to have a story to tell if you haven't survived anything.

Chapter Twenty:
When it Rains, it Pours

A S FATE WOULD HAVE it, once again my world came crashing down on me. I found myself living the adage: "When it rains, it pours." Things were going unbelievably smoothly. I was so busy that I didn't have time to spend any money. Now, that's the kind of problem that any true hustler hopes to have! The only apparent problem was that old boy hadn't called about the Birkens, and my deadline to return them for a refund had passed. I'd been texting him and leaving messages to no avail. I called Tee and asked her if she'd heard anything from him. She said that she would check around.

A problem with my handbag business only arose when the grace period for canceling my order and returning the bags was close to expiring. With my cash on the line, that is a business no-no! If a client had failed to call or make an additional payment, I would be forced to immediately exercise my option to cancel their order, so I could return the items to my vendor. It was a policy I developed to prevent huge losses on my end. Thus, the transaction with 20%

down protected me. When the grace period expired for my clients, I took no joy in keeping their deposits. I was sympathetic to the fact that people ran into hard times and difficulties from overstepping financial boundaries. But when in doubt, I had no choice but to cancel my order and return the merchandise to my seller in order to receive a refund, minus an 8% restocking fee (whatever the hell that meant!).

On top of that, my cash would still be tied up for ten days with the merchant account provider before I received the remainder of my money back.

I began to realize that in business, everyone liked to play with your money, but didn't allow you to play with theirs. Even when you withdrew your own money from an ATM, they charged you a surcharge for the privilege. (Now, that's a hustle!)

No real business person is in the game to make a habit of returning money. So returns often come with penalties to discourage return transactions. If the refund was just a couple thousand dollars, I'd typically have my seller credit my account, rather than issue a refund. I did that to establish good faith that I would be spending the money with them in the near future.

In the case of the Birkin bags, because I was a third-party seller and not an authorized vendor, I was only able to receive the discounts if I paid my vendor up front and in full. That meant that my 11k was on the line. So my belief in this client would put me in a cash squeeze if he didn't come through. It was a good thing that I had built in safeguards and more than one hustle.

***

TEE FINALLY HIT ME back; she told me that the guy had been indicted. I didn't even care to ask for details. I was like, damn, I'd broken one of my rules, trying to make a few thousand dollars, and now had eleven grand of my own money (my dad's money, actually) tied up in two purses that I couldn't use. Big mistake!

That same day, I got a call from one of the girls at the concierge desk from location one. She was telling me that our unit had been raided by the police. Raided, our unit? What the hell did that mean? Kiesha and I rushed over to the location. When we arrived, dozens of people were being escorted out of the building. There must have been 100 young people! I scanned the area and spotted the woman I rented the unit to, along with a younger woman, talking to the police. I walked up and introduced myself as the lease holder and produced the AirBnB renter's contract. It turns out that the aunt had rented the unit for this little heifer, who had just graduated from high school and wanted to have a get-together. It gets worse...they confiscated drugs and alcohol from the premises.

The officer asked me if I wanted to press charges, informing me that it would clear me of any wrongdoing. All that ran through my mind was *the nerve of these white police officers!* Their racist/elitist attitudes were so deeply rooted that it never occurred to them to threaten the white owners of the building, or the workers who let the people into the establishment to begin with. Because I was a young Black woman, they felt comfortable stretching the interpretation of the law to persuade me to press charges. Of course I wasn't going to press charges!

"Press charges for what? Making a bad decision?" I asked with disgust dripping from my tongue.

We both knew that I couldn't be held responsible for anything that occurred. I had a renter's agreement in my hands. That was why they hadn't attempted to arrest me or charged me with anything from the start.

Despite my anger, I couldn't fathom the idea of helping to persecute two Black women for something so trivial. One woman was trying to do something nice for her niece, and the niece was trying to celebrate her accomplishments without considering how things might get out of control. This sounded like an average Friday night in young America to me.

The police were trying to charge the aunt with providing alcohol to minors. (Any charge was good enough, apparently.) This was typical of the insensitive, systemic institutional, social, and racial injustices that were prevalent in our interactions with law enforcement at the time. I was happy to see many of the young men step up to the police, admitting they had brought their own alcohol, in defense of the aunt. As for the drugs, a small amount of marijuana was found on the floor, not in anyone's personal possession. There were no weapons, fights, nor had anyone gotten hurt.

Nevertheless, the situation almost escalated into a riot. With all the current incidents of police shooting unarmed Black men and the uneasy climate between law enforcement and the Black community, the officers decided to just disperse the crowd and leave well enough alone.

Just to be fair, the renters were creating a disturbance. However, it reminded me of the conversation with my political science professor. While it does us no good to play the blame game, damn, when are you going to admit that you help to perpetuate this whack-ass system, started by your ancestors, that has broken a race of people? The system that placed them in the bondage of ignorance and helped to shove boulders into the path of equality?

When are you going to step up and become an agent for change or use your voice to speak truth to your people? It's not about law breakers avoiding consequences. It's about fairness and equality. Black officers are not made to feel comfortable enough to patrol suburbs and consider arresting white mothers and daughters for throwing a rowdy party. Especially one where no one got hurt! I don't have a clear vision of what the necessary change would look like, but I think that I have a right to imagine that someday we will overcome second class citizenship.

America has to stop persecuting the victims of its crimes, by reverse hatred. However, that's a whole other topic for a whole other conversation.

Despite my anger, I felt sympathy for the girl and her aunt. That could have easily been me and a number of my friends when we graduated from high school. While I was upset, I was more concerned about management and the state of my business affairs.

Kiesha and I went up to the unit to assess the situation further. Thank God that the damages were minimal. We locked up the place and left. The next day, when I arrived with a cleaning crew, there was a fluorescent orange eviction notice on the door. I let the workers in and went straight to the leasing office. This white-haired, ultra over the top, arrogant white lady seemed quite pleased to inform me that I had violated the leasing agreement by subleasing the unit and that I had thirty days to move out. She had a printout of my AirBnB profile and my lease contract violations highlighted, inside a folder.

"I don't know about this other location you have listed, but we don't allow AirBnB subleases in our building. This is a clear violation of your lease agreement. You've forfeited your deposit, and your last month's rent will go towards the $10,000 fine for breaking the contract. You will have thirty days to vacate the premises," she declared, with a self-satisfied and condescending smirk on her face.

In my mind, I heard: "That's why we don't like leasing to your kind." She made no mention of the party incident. And in all actuality, there was no need. The subletting of the unit was enough. She had me dead to the wrong. The profile wasn't even in my name, but it had the address and pictures. If I tried to contest it, then she would use the incident. But that made me think... Having a party wasn't grounds for termination. Hmmm?

My thought immediately went to what my dad called "damage control." This was no time to panic.

"You'll be hearing from my lawyers. I'm not somebody to play with!"

That was all I could muster to preserve my dignity as I snatched the folder from her hand and stormed off. No sooner had I arrived back at the apartment when I received a call from the manager of locations # two and three.

In an attempt to cause me even more trouble, this nasty older white woman had called location two to inform them of the AirBnB profile that we had online. Now I was pissed! First of all, this lady had never seen or dealt with me personally. I was the CEO, not the guarantor or the corporate officer who signed the lease agreement for my company. She never had my number and she never called my mother. These crazies had to know one another, and the first one made it personal, while the second one was dumb enough to back her play.

Following the lead of the first hater, the lady from location number two tried to give me the exact same spiel. She had two problems; first, we had announced from the onset our intention to periodically host different guests throughout the year. Thus, under the corporate lease, there were no permanent residents in either unit. Second, she had no proof that I had subleased.

I told her that I would send over a corporate representative and our attorney to straighten things out. She rudely replied that it wasn't necessary because she had already started the lease termination paperwork and would be in touch. Then she hung up. I was really heated now! She was being disrespectful and playing with my money! I had two clients booked for the weekend and scheduled to arrive at two o'clock. That was 3k and $1,800 that I couldn't afford to lose.

I immediately headed over to the building. When I arrived, my key card to the private residential entrance didn't work. I walked around and entered through the public entrance on the hotel side. I headed to the leasing office and spoke with a younger assistant manager, who was cordial and respectful. She informed me that the manager had just left for vacation and wouldn't be back for at least two weeks. She apologized for her boss overstepping her boundaries and told me that she'd been left to deal with someone else's mess. She said that she looked at our contracts and saw no violations, due to each being a corporate lease with no permanent residents. We'd done this purposely with the intention of hosting multiple guests.

The only problem she noted was that whoever provided the initial applications had used the wrong forms. The lady quietly suggested that I leave things the way they were, so I would easily win any suit brought against the building. The last advice she gave me was to file a formal complaint against the manager with headquarters to cover my tracks. Of course, she asked to be left out of it, if it came to that. I assured her that I never bite a hand that fed me.

She recoded my cards and gave me full access again. I thanked her and tipped her for the inconvenience. I'd learned from my father that no gesture expressed gratitude like a tip!

The great thing about the AirBnB lease in this building was that the leasing office was on the hotel side, and management never saw the comings and goings of the residents. Private access and cameras were monitored by security and not managers. By the grace of God, I met with my clients, got them settled in, and the weekend went off without a hitch.

I ended up losing the apartment at location one. As a result, I had to cancel all my remaining bookings and move the furniture into a storage area. Another damn bill and strike against my credit! At least I was still in business, I told myself.

I continued business as usual at location number two for another month without any incidents. I cut checks to pay that month's operating costs, which included rents, bills, and all my people (approx 11k). We grossed about 20k. Not bad for a month, but not as good as before.

I was treading cautiously, so I mostly accepted bookings for three-day weekends. We did twelve days with an average of $1,200 for the penthouse and ten days at $600 for unit two. After I paid down some of my own bills and expenses, I was able to bank about 4k. Nothing to sneeze at, but I needed to do better. This was a 30k investment out the gate.

I figured that the manager must have spoken to the assistant and found that everything was on the level. At least enough to back up off me. As it turned out, things got worse. I foolishly thought this lady had left things alone. She had been able to tell her friend that she harassed me in good conscience, because she had.

Apparently, not enough. As soon as the checks cleared, I got a notice stating that our leases were being terminated. The reason stated was "Violation of leasing contract." I called my attorney and sent over the documents. She looked them over and said we had an easy case. What she meant by that was beyond my legal knowledge and pay grade. However, she suggested that I comply with the order; then we could file a lawsuit. She also warned that it could take years. She advised me to pay the 10k fee on each apartment for breaking the leases, so it wouldn't affect my mother's credit and we would get all that back as well.

I've never been the type to leave anyone hanging, and I definitely wasn't going to ruin the relationship with both of my parents. Mama always jokes, "Hell, you could have given me that 20k and let me worry about my credit, girl."

That night, when I got home from meeting with my lawyer, I figured it was time for me to sit down and figure out how much of my dad's money I had spent. The unadulterated truth. I knew it was a lot. The apartments, furnishings, operational and miscellaneous costs, purses, fines, rental, my apartments, and bills...approx 200k. Not to mention the cost to start up and maintain ABC, as well as Bruh's blunders. All gone! And the majority in less than a year. I was sick. We were broke. All I had left was a few thousand dollars and whatever money was in the business accounts. I felt like a complete failure.

Chapter Twenty-One:
You Better Tell Him or I Will

AS JAY Z WOULD say, "It was all good just a week ago." After finding myself at rock bottom, I stopped taking my dad's calls. Before I knew it, I was back home on my mother's couch. I was really flat broke. Not just temporarily out of cash, with something in the works. Worse than that, I'd not only squandered all the money, I'd lost the apartment as well. Can you imagine? The fabulous Lauren Washington, broke and homeless!

The only people I shared this traumatic phase of my life with were my mother, my cousin Kiesha, and Jay. People who had known me since before I achieved my Hollywood status. I knew they would still have my back, no matter what. Nevertheless, it still hurt to have fallen from grace and to be seen by them in such a deplorable state. I went into a serious mental funk. It was difficult to eat or sleep. I lost about twenty pounds. My mama often joked that she thought my hair was falling out as well. I didn't find that funny at all! Anyone who knows me knows that I'm very vain about my hair. I won't admit it much, but I smile inside when someone asks me who does my weave. My hair was all I had left to my name, and my mom thought it was cute to joke like that!

Anyway...Kiesha offered to take care of me and let me stay at her apartment. I graciously declined. I told her I needed to be at my mama's house. It would have added insult to injury to have to sleep on her couch, broke, while she made boss moves. Like a real trooper, she still came by every day to check on me before she went to work. My ex-boyfriend Jay and I had maintained a healthy relationship through our breakup, and he came by to check up on me as well. When I told him about everything, he didn't rub it in, like I thought he would. Instead, he offered to help me get back on my feet. I quickly declined.

I knew Jay, and men have a way of feeling entitled and making you feel like you owe them something when they do something for you. Plus, maybe I was a little paranoid about what position I would put myself back into, now that I had declared my independence.

I will never forget when he said, "You'd better tell that man you spent all his money."

The way he said it, you would think that he was more afraid than I was, but for totally different reasons. He sure wasn't about to take the blame for me. I was thinking to myself, *Damn, could you tell him for me?*

Anybody, but me!

***

ONE THING ABOUT my mom and dad that sets them apart from typical parents is that they have their own code of ethics about secrets. For me and my siblings, if you know any of their secrets, you'd better take them to the grave. That doesn't mean they will keep your secrets from each other. They have no such loyalty to you. They will, however, give you a chance to break the news first.

Because I wasn't taking my father's calls, he was calling my mother more often. Like every day. Mind you, until this point, this man and I had never gone a day without speaking. Sometimes five to ten times in a day. Now, there was absolutely zero communication.

I began to consider things like: *What could he be thinking is wrong? Is he worried? Is he mad? Does he know? Did my mom tell him?* (This was one of the times when I wish she had.)

I knew eventually I would have to tell him myself. I didn't expect to get off the hook that easily! I just wasn't ready to face the music right then.

As fate would have it, one Sunday morning, he called while Mama was cooking breakfast for Maddy and me. She put the phone on speaker when she answered and asked my little sister to take her food to her room. She looked at me and said, "Okay, that's enough of this shit! Either you tell him right now or I'm going to!"

"Tell me what?" my dad asked calmly.

Looking back, I realize he was much too calm and collected for this to have been a surprise. To spare me further embarrassment and shame, I'll just give you the short version of the dialogue.

So I'm on the phone crying, telling my dad that we were broke. I've spent all of his money. He was silent the entire time I spoke, and the silence was killing me. His unspoken thoughts were far more frightening than anything he could have said. If you know my dad, he's never short on words. He's always barking orders or breaking something down to us.

"What do you mean MY money is gone?" he finally asked in a menacing tone that sent chills through my body.

I was sobbing hard at this point from all the guilt.

"It's all gone!" I managed between even harder sobs.

"What the f@#k are you crying for? I'm the one who should be crying. Now I have nothing. You took our financial independence. You took my and your brother's attorney fees. But even worse, I can no longer trust you. So I'm the one who lost everything, and if I ain't crying, you ain't got a right to cry either. So shut that shit up!"

I'd heard him talk to other people like that, but he'd never spoken to me that way. I was so hurt that I just hung up the phone on him. He called right back, and I didn't answer. I was too hurt and ashamed. I felt betrayed and abandoned, so I refused to talk. My immaturity was kicking in. I was trying to find a justification for my actions. In pain, I concluded that if he wanted to talk to me like that, then fine, we didn't have to have a relationship. That attitude didn't last long. Somehow, in the midst of him calling my mom back, they got into a heated argument, and I felt even worse. My actions were now coming between my parents, whom I had never witnessed say anything bad about each other.

"All right, Leroy, that's enough," my mother said, followed by a long silence on her part.

Apparently, she was listening to what he was saying. The time on the fifteen-minute call must have been running out, because she told my dad, "Just call back later. She'll be here. She ain't got nowhere to go."

Needless to say, as soon as the phone call ended, I got an earful from my mother. She cursed me out and told me to never hang up the phone on my father again! She made sure that I knew that I was the one who wronged him and that I would have to take my lashes standing up! *What the hell does that mean, anyway?* I was thinking,

"Damn, whose side are you on?" As the days went by, I was trying to prepare for the inevitable conversation. I recalled vividly the last words he'd uttered when I told him about the loan I'd taken: "Don't spend a dime of my money..." Those words had been haunting me ever since the first time I went into his cash, trying to maintain things, after spending every dime I had.

I hadn't been out of the house for weeks, trying to muster up the energy to face the world. It was bad enough that I didn't like the sight of my own reflection in the mirror. I saw none of the "boss chick" I'd been masquerading as. In fact, I spent many hours in a daze, wishing that my life was just a bad dream. I was desperate, and no one could have understood how devastated I was.

I knew the main question would be, "How did I foolishly blow all the money?" I anticipated his call each day, only to suffer anxiety again the next day, awaiting my trial by fire.

To my amazement, he hadn't called me or my mom for over a week. Now, I was really worried. Had my actions somehow set off another chain of events? Could my father be sitting in the hole or gotten into a violent confrontation because of his anger over what I'd done? Now that I was getting past the guilt, misery, and shame, in preparation to face the music, clarity started to kick in. I was finally starting to understand things on a deeper level. I began to recalibrate and get my bearings back, so I could focus.

Truthfully, it was the first time that I had the opportunity to backtrack my steps and really think about where I had spent all that money. How I managed to let things get out of control. I analyzed how everything had spiraled out of control so quickly!

I asked myself, *What ultimately knocked me off my feet? That was what I needed to identify.* After a deep self-analysis, I concluded three things for certain. First, I had to fix things with my father.

Second, I was going to get my money right again, soon! And third, I would never allow this to happen again. Falling off had been crippling and embarrassing. It was especially humbling given that I'd spent my entire life formulating a strategy for success, and to make my dad proud, simultaneously.

***

THE MOMENT OF TRUTH finally arrived. My dad called. He didn't say, "Hello" or "Hey, baby." There were no niceties or subtleties. When my father is upset, he gets straight to the point. This was one of those times when he had every right to be mad.

"Do you know where you went wrong?" he asked, far too calmly for someone whose daughter had just told him a week prior that he was bankrupt.

Another factor I hadn't considered was that, nine times out of ten, he'd already calculated and countered every way the conversation could go. I knew that I was unprepared for what he had in mind. I said, "Yes" and tried to explain what I thought was the error in my actions. I intended to be a grown woman about the whole thing and earn his respect again.

He cut me off mid-sentence. "I'm not talking about no f@#king money, Pooh!"

I could hear the anger in his voice, but at least he called me Pooh, right?

"Money will never come between us! You almost f@#ked up our relationship. I needed to know that I could trust you under any circumstances or conditions," he spat with righteous indignation.

"I know, Dad," I responded with my voice cracking and tears starting to flow down my face.

"You know what?" he asked sarcastically.

"I messed up, Dad!"

He could hear the weakness in my voice and said, "Don't you start that weak ass crying shit! I'm serious. I don't wanna hear it."

Then he went on about relationships and trust. He then defined our relationship, before speaking more in depth about loyalty, honor, respect, and boundaries. I waited for him to make me explain what I'd done with the cash. I was flabbergasted that he didn't even ask what happened to his money.

My thought process was all thrown off! None of this conversation resembled the normal routine that we went through when I made a mistake. Suddenly, the lightbulb went on and I quickly realized this wasn't a normal situation. Our relationship was at a pivotal point, and what I said and did at this moment would determine where our relationship went from this moment forward.

Trying to be a big girl, I mustered the nerve to ask, "So are you going to forgive me?"

I really just wanted to move on and get us back into the space we'd always shared. I needed his forgiveness, or all the plans I was formulating to redeem us, were in vain.

"I've already forgiven you or we wouldn't be talking," he answered simply.

That answer was like hearing a judge say "probation" for a robbery charge.

The next words out of his mouth were to give me an attorney's phone number. He told me to call her at nine a.m., his time, and not a second later! This was a demand. I had absolutely no idea what he had in mind for me. Only a man like my dad could interject something as completely random as that into a conversation, and I instinctively knew that there was something important behind it. There were no other instructions or explanations, and I knew better than to ask.

When I got off the phone, my mother asked, "What did he say?"

"Ma, he didn't even ask about the money." I explained the conversation with a million thoughts running through my mind. Just when I thought I had him figured out, he surprised me again.

It never ceased to amaze me how well my mother knew my father. At this time, they hadn't been together in over twenty years, but she easily assured me that the whole issue was about something other than what I thought.

"This ain't about no damn money. Back in the day, I counted ten times the money you lost in an hour for your father."

Now, the secrets were coming out. I was suddenly more interested in hearing what she knew about my father's dark days. I had never heard my mother talking about my daddy's past life. The stories I heard were mostly from uncles and other family members, who weren't as concerned with protecting my dad's reputation.

"What do you mean? Are all those rumors about my dad true?" I asked, thirsty for a deeper glimpse into where I got my genetics from.

"No!" she exclaimed quickly, shutting me down.

"Don't worry about all that. That's a whole other life and a different time. He is so much more than what he used to be. And that's all you need to know about your father."

I determined that it must have hurt my mom too badly to discuss the past because she never really talked about it. Obviously, my dad was taken away from her, as well as us. That had to be devastating, considering the life they shared before his incarceration. They had been together since high school.

Maybe she suffered from the same stolen dreams as my dad, and I'd never taken the time to consider that. Perhaps that was why they remained so close over the years and the reason why no other man had ever been able to recreate the same bond. Something in her expression told me not to press on. From time to time, she would say something that validated that she once had a leading role in the movie and not just a cameo appearance. I don't care what anyone says, I've never seen a nun married to a mobster. I'm just saying.

"You just hurt and disappointed him really bad," she suggested afterwards.

"I know, Ma." She didn't have to rub it in.

"If I know your dad, that phone call to the lawyer is another one of his tests. He likes to play mind games. If you're gonna keep up with him, you better sharpen your skills, little girl! You're in the big leagues now, and you better bring your 'A' game, as they call it. But if you play your cards right, everything will be okay. You just cannot ever betray his trust again. As much as he loves you, he will still cut you off forever. He has serious trust issues and he loves hard, Lauren. You only got a second chance because he loves your little ass more than anything in this world."

Still hoping to pry out just a little more about my dad, I asked what she meant by "trust issues."

"Your father is a very complicated man. He's always been smart, handsome, fearless, and has a huge heart. He always had more than everyone else, because he went harder to get it. And he was more loyal to them than they were to him. That made people jealous of him. His damn arrogance didn't help. Back then, one of his biggest downfalls was that he took everything to heart and was far too serious about life. When people underestimated him, he made them learn quickly, and most of the time harshly and without mercy. Especially for betrayal. But he's human and he makes mistakes too. So yes, he has trust issues."

It seemed like she was talking in riddles, and my honest opinion just happened to state the obvious.

"It seems like he always trusted you, even now," I suggested, wondering why.

Maybe it was my tone, or she read my mind, because she instantly came back with, "Because I'm trustworthy! I never cheated on your father. Never stole from him, or betrayed his trust in any kind of way."

Damn, that didn't make me feel any better.

"You'll fix this and you'll make other mistakes along the way. But I'm confident you won't make this one again," she said with a smirk and suppressed laughter that surfaced when she said something slick.

I didn't say anything slick in response. Unlike my father's meaningless physical threats, my mama was right there in front of me. If she chose to slap me, there was nothing I could do about it. On the other hand, there was nothing like my mother's reassurance when it came to my father. I almost asked her to put in a good word for me. She and my grandmother were the only two women who could tell my dad when his hat was too small. But in reality, I knew that no one could fix this problem but me.

To make a long story short: This was a defining moment and crucial phase in my life. Bad money management skills and the inability to overcome the challenges and obstacles that life was throwing at me had caused me to make one bad decision after another. My advice to anyone who is experiencing any difficulties in life (and trust me, you will), be it mentally, physically, or emotionally: You need to get some help before it gets out of hand. Never be afraid to ask for help. There is power in facing the truth, but the key is getting the right help.

***

INDEED THIS WAS ONE of the most embarrassing and difficult times of my life. We all have them. As my father would say: "The most important thing is learning to overcome difficulties and not letting those moments defeat us or define us."

I would advise you to never allow what you are going through to cause you to treat others indifferently. We never have the right to mistreat others who haven't done anything wrong to us. We don't have a right to cheat, deceive, or take advantage of others because someone victimizes us. More importantly, we have to reconcile our differences and rectify our errors, especially with the people we love. I will never again betray my father's trust. It seemed like it hurt me more than it did him.

On a personal note: Dad, even though you made it easy for us to move on, I'm still deeply sorry about my actions!

Now I know that even when I can't see the beauty of the wisdom in his tutelage, it still exists. Those growing pains helped me to become the woman I am today. To me, that's the magic of true parenting.

Chapter Twenty-Two:
Second Chances

THE LESSONS I LEARNED from this period in my life have proven to be invaluable.

Failures and hardships are a part of the journey that prepares you for success. In time, I have come to truly understand what my dad meant when he wrote: "I have learned over the years that the furrows and ridges of inconsistency and pain are the contours that give life its meaning. I can rage at the heavens...but I must simultaneously thank them for the blessed gifts..."

In simplest terms: Without those experiences I wouldn't be the woman I am today!

I had finally patched things up with my dad. Deep down, I believe that my mother had something to do with how easy it was, but then again, I can never underestimate my father's reasons for anything. One thing was certain: he would never allude to any conversation that they may have had about me.

Things were starting to turn around in my life. I attributed it to positive thoughts and energy. I was happier now than when I had money to spend. That's how I knew the lessons of failure and family were real. I was just happy to still be a part of the unit that created and sustained the young lady who made the bad choices.

I was wondering why he wanted me to call this attorney. I couldn't even begin to imagine why. I called at nine a.m. precisely, with my mother's words still ringing in my ears: "It's probably another test."

That only reinforced to me that there was no room for failure. The introduction and subtleties lasted no longer than a minute, tops.

"I can't wait to meet you...I've heard so much about you...I need you to come to Atlanta tomorrow." Straight to the point. "Your dad needs you to sign these papers. Call me as soon as you get in, and have a safe trip."

I guess she knew that I had no choice but to agree. Never mind what I might have going on, the demand was to be there! She sent me the flight confirmation number, and told me that a car would be there to pick me up and not to bother to rent a room.

I got the impression that this woman was more than just an attorney or friend. She seemed to move too uniformly with my dad's program. Like someone who had years of being involved in his affairs. But just who was she, and why had he never mentioned her to me before?

As soon as I got off the phone, my mama was right there in my face.

"Well, what did she say?" she asked with a desperate curiosity.

How in hell did this lady know I was talking to a female? I wondered. Did she know the lady? Had she dealt with her before? My mind raced with questions, but I was careful to follow the example of my parents and not reveal too much!

"You tell me--what're you and Daddy cooking up on?" I shot back at her.

"Don't be getting smart with me! I heard her voice through the phone with your little smart ass!" she snapped back.

Okay, I was tripping, but she got me together real quick. I guess I was always secretive when it came to me and my dad's dealings (keeping things close to the vest). It didn't matter if we were in a good place or not. My mom knew this about me, but seemed to always find a way to remind me that she was my mother, not one of my girls, and not to get it twisted! Point taken.

***

I LANDED IN ATLANTA and headed downtown, wondering what this meeting could possibly be about. I hoped that nothing was wrong with my dad. As soon as I made it to the building, I dialed the number, and she picked up on the other end.

"Hey, I'm downstairs," I announced as I approached the security station near the elevators.

"I thought that was you. Look over to your left," said the voice from the other end of the phone.

The attorney was already standing in the lobby. She didn't look like what I expected. I was pleasantly surprised to see that she was definitely my father's type, if he had one. Light-skinned, jazzy, with sophisticated hair, nails, and makeup. In fact, her attire and mannerisms spoke of high class. Obviously she was smart; she was an attorney. I sensed that she was a few years older than my parents, although she didn't look it.

She attempted to break the ice. "Hi, I'm Monica, and you're Pooh, right?"

"Yes, I'm Lauren. Nobody calls me Pooh but my dad."

"Oh, I'm sorry, Ms. Washington," she corrected herself in a friendly, yet sarcastic tone.

I immediately thought about two things my mother had told me before I left. One, this was one of my father's tests. And two, you catch more flies with honey. So while I was deciding if I liked this woman, or feared what she represented between me and my dad, I checked myself.

"I'm sorry. I didn't mean to come off rude. That's just a special name that only me and dad use. Lauren is fine."

"No apology necessary. Lauren it is."

"But if you're special to my dad, which you must be, then you can call me Pooh," I said, trying to bait her into giving me more information about her and my dad's relationship.

"Oh no, it's not like that. I wish I had met your father thirty years ago, before I met my husband's sorry ass, or he met your mother. But that's a whole other lifetime," she said in a wistful tone.

"What exactly do you do for my dad?"

"I'll tell you everything you want to know over dinner. Let's go up to my office and take care of some business first, then get you something to eat before we get you settled in. I'm starving myself."

She had navigated around my questions expertly. I had to remind myself that she was an attorney. They were in the business of extracting information from people--not being tricked into divulging it. This woman was growing on me quickly, but I wasn't sold just yet.

I could tell she was a boss. Her firm wasn't as big as the one that Ley took me to in New York, but her name was on the wall as a partner. Upstairs, her office was beautiful. Huge leather chairs, a conference table and sitting area, all in her own private office suite, separated from her partners by real walls. I should have expected an adventure after the conversation with my dad. He was both understanding and mysterious, and I was still on a rollercoaster of emotions.

After a few pleasantries, she pulled a phone from her drawer, placed it on her desk, and looked at her watch. Almost simultaneously the phone rang, and she answered.

"Hey you...I'm good! She's right here, and everything you said she was. Let me put you on speaker," Monica said enthusiastically.

I had an idea that my dad was on the other end of the line, but I noticed that she didn't push a button to accept the call. On occasion, my dad had access to things and devices that others in his position didn't, so it didn't surprise me.

"Hey, baby!" said the familiar voice.

"Heeey, Dad!" I responded excitedly.

"So you've met Monni. She's an entertainment and estate attorney who has been a friend for years. I'm cashing in some of my stocks, bonds, and a life insurance policy that you're the beneficiary of. I was saving them for a rainy day, and it looks like that day has arrived. We need a fresh start. Can I trust you to manage these affairs properly?" he asked.

I answered "yes," with tears streaming down my face. I didn't know if they were tears of happiness or shame, but I was definitely feeling overwhelmed with emotions. Monica handed me some tissues and put her fingers to her lips, signaling me to try to keep my composure. It appeared that she was aware of my dad's contempt for weakness as well.

We spoke for about twenty minutes as he instructed us on what he wanted me to do. As soon as Monica started to explain how much money he had left, he interrupted, and she caught on immediately. Some things weren't to be discussed on the phone, even on a personal line. There were agencies that listened to EVERY call, regardless of the origin, and they weren't the intended recipients of the privileged information…or maybe he didn't want me to know?

"Hey, I love y'all, and God willing, I'll talk to you later," he said, and hung up.

At that point, Monica presented me with the paperwork I needed to sign. She and my dad had clearly coordinated this thing to the letter. It appeared that I was signing everything over to her. Why her? I asked myself. Beyond that, I'd never heard my dad tell ANY woman outside of the family that he loved them. Who was this woman to him?

Some might say that I was worried about the wrong thing, but I was determined to find out when we had our dinner date that night.

As it turned out, Monica was just my daddy's attorney and great friend. She told me about their history and how he had brought her a few big-name clients, back in the day, such as my second cousin Andre Rison and his then girlfriend, Lisa "Left Eye" Lopes of TLC. Apparently, he had given her some good advice about the benefits of starting her own firm and invested in her. That had been the springboard to her success.

They became good friends, and she managed a few of my dad's investments and his portfolio. At least that's the story she gave me. However, what I did know about my dad was that it was hard to earn his trust. There had to be a deeper level to their acquaintance than what met the eye. But I guess who and what she was to him wasn't that important in the grand scheme of things. What was important was that he trusted me to meet this woman and wanted me to learn something from her. Thus, I reminded myself to pay attention to all the details. I made a mental note that she would be a good person to keep in touch with.

She took me to a high-rise apartment building off Peachtree, not too far away from her downtown office. "I heard you like high-rises," she remarked smartly.

We both got a laugh from that inside joke.

"You can stay here anytime you're in town. This used to be your father's, twenty something years ago, before I bought it from him. Of course I redecorated it to my liking. Since my children are all grown up and my husband died a while back, I spend most of my time here, instead of the big ole house on the golf course. I haven't been able to find love again. Plus, as I'm getting older, I hate the hour-long commute from the country club into the city. Those are all stories for another time."

She set two glasses on the bar to pour us drinks, and I held up my hand. My father taught me a long time ago that drinking or using substances is a sign of weakness. You never displayed your guilty pleasures or weaknesses in front of strangers. Especially people of power.

We talked for another hour about my life, ABC, and my mistakes. Her life and her mistakes. I felt like we genuinely bonded and she could have been one of my aunties or something. I noticed that she never touched her glass, either.

She reached in her purse and handed me an envelope as she got up to leave. She was headed home and leaving me access to her high-rise.

"I have a full day tomorrow. This is from your dad. I'm sure your experiences will help you navigate the pitfalls this time. Don't be afraid to make mistakes, but take calculated risks," she said, as if she had the utmost confidence in me. She then added, "Don't forget, I'm here for you too, if you ever need me."

I thanked her for the hospitality and for remaining loyal to my father for such a long time, and told her that it was a pleasure to have met.

"You don't have to thank me for that. Good friends are hard to come by, and your father is a man of integrity and honor. He was there for me in some of my darkest hours, and believe it or not, I learned a lot from him. You'd be surprised. However, at this phase of his life, his only focus is you. Lauren, he loves you more than anything in this world. I admire your relationship and I wish I had something nearly as special with any of my children. You're everything I imagined and more, so the honor and the pleasure was all mine."

   *NOTE TO SELF: IT was only money to my dad. Therefore I was able to learn to get to the root of the problem so I didn't make the same mistakes again. It took a great deal of mental fortitude and love for him to look past the act, get to the reason, and make it a lesson, as only he can do! It all starts with identifying the root of the issue; but we can never do it while making excuses or playing the blame game. I might have been a little bit salty about the way my life was playing out in real time, but that was no excuse for what I did to my best friend...my father!

Chapter Twenty-Three:
Ley

A S IF THINGS COULDN'T get any worse...I'll never forget the call. It was early morning, two days after Christmas, and Paris was blowing up my phone. We hadn't spoken since she left to move in with Ley. They had since moved back to Atlanta and shared an apartment in Buckhead.

I finally answered, and all I heard was deep sobbing.

"Paris, what's wrong? What's going on?" I asked in a panic. No reply. "Paris, you're scaring me! Are you all right?"

"Lauren, Ley is dead!"

I couldn't utter a sound. I didn't believe what I was hearing. An overwhelming sadness overcame me. We were once sisters, and no matter what we were going through at the time, I couldn't imagine her being dead. That shit was permanent. Final. We were all so young. Who died before they got married or had children? None of us had reached our ultimate goals or the climax of our potential. Dead?

We were still chasing our dreams and searching for fulfillment. This was not the way I wanted or imagined that our friendship would end. We didn't even get the chance to say that we were sorry. That our differences were too petty to break our pact. That we still loved each other. Goodbye.

Paris finally calmed down enough to tell me what happened. Ley was on one of her secret rendezvous. She'd met a dude from Baton Rouge, Louisiana, who was some kind of baller. He must have crossed the wrong people back home. They went to visit his family and were killed. The police found them dead in a Wendy's parking lot. The dude had been shot twice in the back of the head. Ley was shot in the neck and bled out. The detectives called Paris because she was the last number dialed from Ley's phone. They believed that it was a hit and not a robbery, because Ley still had rolls of cash in her purse, which was lying on the floor, and all of her jewelry. Several cameras caught the images of the murder. A man simply walked up to the car and got into the back seat. There were several muzzle flashes. He got out the car and walked off.

We heard they caught him. I'm sure there was more information that they couldn't share with us. I never asked who the shooter was or what happened to him. I don't handle death well, at all. My dad says it's because I don't have a good relationship with my Lord— that as I develop one, I'll be able to relate to life and death a little better. That these things won't affect me as harshly. But I can't imagine a time when my relationship with God will help me master the emotions concerning death. I'll never get used to the loss of life.

That whole day I watched hundreds of videos of our time together and our matching Pacman Ghost tattoos to commemorate our pact to achieve excellence. The videos captured great moments with our friends. I shared them with everyone, and they posted and shared them in memory of Ley.

It was a good thing I was already at my mama's house, because I didn't want to be alone.

My dad called, and I told him what had happened. He told me that he'd had a bad dream about me and the girls getting into a fatal car accident where one of us didn't make it. In the dream, he and my mother were trying to find out which of us it was. The doctors said that Paris and I had gotten burned really badly, but Ley had died. He said that he'd never awakened with such sadness. Then he told me about the advice he had gotten when Uncle Pruitt had been killed. He also made sure to remind me of what was ahead.

"Pooh, it ain't gonna be easy, but we're going to get through this. You can't afford to fall into a funk. You never know how long it will last...a day, a week, a month, a year, a lifetime. When that happens, you ain't no good to yourself or no one else." I knew he was right. I was glad to have him at that moment. He really helped me to process things.

***

258

LEY HAD A BEAUTIFUL funeral in January 2020. Her makeup was well done, and she was dressed like she would have wanted to be seen for her last appearance. I couldn't help but think that she looked like she was asleep, and I expected her to wake up at any moment.

While I had spoken to her mom and sister Taj when Ley and I lived together, the funeral was the first time that I had seen them since high school. We hugged and silently acknowledged that this moment was about Ley. They invited me to come over to the house after the burial. I nodded my agreement to be there.

So many people turned out to send Ley off. I had no idea that she had so many friends or lovers. I imagined Ley looking down on us and laughing: "Yeah, I got y'all asses this time!"

Paris, Neha, and I rode together to the cemetery. It was sad to say the least, and the burial finalized things for me. I never thought that this would be the way I'd see her for the last time.

On the flight home, I vowed to never take life, or a friendship, for granted again. I wouldn't hold grudges or allow other people's pettiness or selfishness to affect me negatively. I promised myself that I would go ten times as hard as before. There would be no more time for games or mediocrity. I would finish what we started by making ABC an organization that would change and save young people's lives.

In memory of a life cut short: Ley, I'm sorry that we never got a chance to resolve our petty squabbles one more time! I've never judged you because you were my sister. My friend...until we meet again. You are gone, but will never be forgotten! Rest in peace, lil sis!

Chapter Twenty-Four:
COVID

2020 WAS THE WORST start of any year that I could remember. I could list a litany of tragedies that began with Ley's funeral. Kobe and Gigi died in a helicopter crash, and the COVID pandemic hit the world in early March and scared us all half to death. The world seemed to be ending.

***

AFTER ALL THE TRAGIC moments that took place prior to 2020, the coronavirus or COVID-19 struck early in the year and changed the world we knew. In its novelty stages, the virus was something that we (society) just weren't prepared for. By mid-2020, positive results and death rates were skyrocketing, with no signs of slowing down. Not only was the country shut down, but the rest of the world as well. There was no doubt that this thing was beyond serious. Without outright declaring Martial Law, citizens of the world, not just America, were ordered to remain confined to our homes. The consensus was that the virus, without hosts to infect, would subside and possibly die off. The government politely called it a "shelter at home" quarantine period.

Our schools, businesses, churches, clubs, and sporting arenas were shut down, and the streets resembled a post-apocalyptic ghost town! They even distinctively labeled professionals who were necessary to maintain hospitals, law enforcement, and other essential services "frontline workers."

Most Americans, myself included, had no idea of what to do. The poor, urban areas were hit the hardest. You couldn't help but to think that there was possibly a conspiracy element at play. All we could do was hope and pray that neither we, nor our families, would become fatalities.

As fate would have it, while no one in my family had fallen victim to the virus, my grandfather LeRoy Washington, Sr. (my dad's dad) passed away in September 2020 from other health complications. That was really hard on my father. They were really close. As I mentioned earlier, unlike the majority of young Black men I've encountered who were raised by women, my dad will tell you that there was never a time when his father wasn't in his life.

Grandpa had been in a fully accommodated assisted-living home for the past couple of years, since he had a heart attack. We believe he died from loneliness. When the shutdown occurred, none of my uncles or family members were allowed to visit him, and his health took a turn for the worse. My father took the whole ordeal a lot better than I imagined he would. He said, "From God we came, and to him we must all return."

The thing that he was most upset about was that he didn't get a chance to tell his dad that he loved him one more time and that he wished he had been a better son. Because of COVID, the country shut down funerals. We had to improvise, but he had a beautiful memorial service outside at the burial site.

Shortly thereafter, in October of 2020, my father was the first person of anyone I knew to contract the deadly virus. Of all people, it would have to be my father! I was worried and angry at the same time!

It was no secret that our notoriously broken prison system didn't care enough about the men we love to provide decent health care. There was nothing in their playbook that concerned the health of my father. In Michigan, they didn't even entertain "Compassionate Release" for elderly or high-risk convicts, like other states and the Feds had. Most prisoners didn't even receive proper masks. They were forced to make their own from old clothing or bed linens. It took for celebrities like Jay-Z, Meek Mill, Robert Kraft, Kim Kardashian, and many other powerful people to donate millions of N95 masks for prisoners.

My dad suffered every symptom of COVID except extreme respiratory failure (which is the most deadly). Fortunately, his healthy lifestyle and eating habits proved to be his saving grace. He hadn't used any drugs or drink alcohol in nearly thirty years. His physical health and mental fortitude was superior to many of the prisoners and certainly men in the streets. He survived and bounced back with a vengeance.

While it was natural for me to worry, I nearly cried when he called me and boastfully declared, "Hey, don't worry about me. I'm good. I didn't survive those mean streets and two and a half decades of prison to let a virus kill me!"

We both had a good laugh, and the strength in his voice assured me that my hero was still as much a Superman as always. I did some extensive research and learned that fewer than one percent of the people who contracted the virus, died from it. That made me feel a little better. But being more informed made me more suspicious as well. I really began to wonder if this was all some ruse that the government was pulling on the people.

In the following year, I finally contracted the virus, along with three-fourths of the entire planet—even those who were so-called vaccinated. My father also contracted the virus a second time. Thankfully, he was asymptomatic and didn't have so much as a sneeze that time.

***

FOR THE NEXT TWO years, the world was under siege. A new normal that changed everyday life was ushered in. Millions of people died. My heart goes out to everyone who lost a loved one. In this period of loss, isolation, financial depression, and despair, grief and sadness took center stage. Depression has always been a tough road to navigate. It can be triggered by a lot less than the death of a loved one. I can tell you from firsthand experience that everyone experiences grief differently.

There are several stages of an individual's spiral. Grief or depression is a serious subject that should be handled with care. If you feel like you need help dealing with a loss, I encourage you to seek the help of a medical professional. If you or someone you know is contemplating suicide, please don't ignore the signs. Call the National Suicide Hotline at 988. Talking these things out is a great way to gain a different perspective on the value of living another day.

***

BEING CONFINED TO OUR homes compelled us to take a hard look at the core question of "our failing humanity towards one another." People were forced to shelter at home and spend time with others in a way we had not done before. This kind of social constraint definitely had an effect on people.

Before, there had always been jobs, school, activities, and other factors that gave us breathing room. The forced interaction of the COVID lockdown actually strengthened emotional bonds and drew some people closer. The adverse effect was that many others discovered that they weren't as compatible as they had believed, and reinforced underlying reasons to end their relationships. As a result, the breakup and divorce rate was higher than at any other time in history.

Being restricted to their homes drove Americans crazy! Especially the youth. All of our pent-up energy needed an outlet.

During this time, White police officers continued killing unarmed Black men. When they killed an unarmed George Floyd by kneeling on his windpipe for over eight minutes, while being filmed, it provoked Americans to release a shockwave of longtime frustrations into the world. This backlash against oppression set the tone for change in America.

Despite curfews and "stay-at-home" orders, people took to the streets in protest. But this time was different. Unlike before, when angry urban mobs simply burned buildings and cars or looted businesses, the attack was more focused. Many of the protests were centered around government buildings, police stations, and even the nation's Capital.

More impactful was the fact that White people joined the cause to say that "enough was enough!" I want to believe that all people are inherently good, but I know better. I believe the protests were the response to a mixture of blatant disregard for human life and the boredom and anxiety of an oppressed nation. In other words, our agendas aligned and created the perfect storm.

Those who weren't being shot down were aggravated by being told that they had little or no freedom to make decisions about how they spent their days during COVID. Either way, the assistance was appreciated. They say that: "The enemy of an enemy is a friend."

To be candid, I can see racism being the mindset of a dying breed. However, there will always be elitists, regardless of race. I'm not the moral police, so I'm less concerned with how people think and more impressed by how they act. Regardless of their motivations.

My father said that his grandmother once told him: "You need to be thanking God, Allah, or whomever you worship, for the white man. Niggas didn't free themselves from slavery. It wasn't until them good Christian white folk took up guns against their own kind that we got free. So all of them ain't bad."

I would like to have seen the look on his face when she hit him with those undeniable facts. I was reminded during my lifetime that the racial divide I've experienced isn't as deeply rooted as the "idea" of a racial divide. We seem to all be looking for the Boogie Man when dealing with other races in America.

When we ignore the differences of culture, we readily find commonality and purpose. My dad said that he didn't really understand the truth of the statement until later in his life. As I stated earlier, I was never so politically invested, and my parents never allowed us to participate in protests because they were too dangerous. My father likes to point out that the difference between a peaceful protest and a riot is a "heartbeat." I've just never been interested in marching or complaining. I'd rather expend my energy by working on solutions. That's doing my part.

***

I HAVE TO GIVE it to my dad for his ability to see past the obvious. His unorthodox education, courtesy of the School of Hard Knocks, made him look for the "purpose" behind any action. After recovering from COVID, he paid close attention to the actions of the government, which indicated that their agenda was primarily to enrich themselves. Trillions of dollars were allocated for business and personal financial relief, medical assistance relief, and economic stimulus. Although most of my constituents aren't big fans of Donald Trump, they were certainly grateful for their $3200 piece of the action. I didn't turn the money down either, but my proficiency at basic math kept me from celebrating my windfall.

Just as a side note: Let's just take the sum of 7 trillion dollars. If you gave 350 million Americans just $10,000 that would only be... (Using my fingers...subtract the two...carry the one...divided by 350...) Ummm, nowhere near even $4 trillion. So "We the People" got the crumbs and the big players got the cake... As usual!

In terms of America's greatest heists, COVID-19 was a classic. It wasn't nearly as deadly as it was purported to be, but it's apparent that propaganda goes a long way. Especially when people are worried about dying. Who had time to concern themselves about a few decimal points that the government may have been moving around?

Even more ingenious was the fact that the money moved in 350 million directions. No one could follow or pinpoint just how much money moved in which direction—especially when there were thirty different agencies tasked with "allocating" funds, with more springing up all the time. The State of Emergency Acts allowed states to access previously withheld funds. In some cases, billions. In these times, the rich get the steak and the poor get the crumbs ($3200 worth of crumbs).

***

I TRIED TO DEBATE my dad's conspiratorial mind, but it played out right in front of my eyes. Once again, he was right. We didn't know all the angles, but that's how the game goes. When a reporter asked Donald Trump about all the fraudulent claims for unemployment made by people and businesses, his response was shockingly dismissive, to say the least.

"I see that you have on a ring. Did you and your spouse get some money? DID YOU GET A CHECK?"

When the reporter replied "yes," he stated "Then what are you talking about? Our concerns are the needs of the American people and the economy. We'll bring all the scammers to justice later. Don't let that be your concern right now."

I had to say to myself, "Spoken like a true gangster. Well played, Commander-in-Chief." The reporter definitely caught the message: "You're worried about the wrong thing, and you'd better shut up before I ruin your life."

My dad says that he doesn't like Trump the President, but he loves Trump the Crook. He finds the fact that he shows no regard for bureaucrats or citizens, equally, commendable. "Trump's God is the Almighty dollar. People like him will bait your hook with a fish, so that they can catch a shark." This kind of "overplay-for-the-underlay" scheme is when one gives a little in order to steal a lot.

They say that you can learn a lot from a dummy. Imagine what you can learn from the smart. Using the strategy employed by Big Brother (in a business sense), all we need is a little to start our journey to getting a lot.

***

IT WAS AT THIS time that my dad "tied my shoes" on how to get to my bag during disasters. As he explained to me, it was during these times that the government released surplus funds to qualified businesses for regional cleanup and control measures. If you offered a product, service, or even professional advice that aligned with their agenda, they would gladly give you the money to do it!

If you were smart, you watched the trend of successful business models and got in where you fit in. I was especially motivated to step up my game when Jeff Bezos boldly announced that: "Amazon was built for a pandemic." His company grossed trillions and skyrocketed his own personal net worth to nearly $200 billion. *Forbes Magazine* even created a title for a wealthy person who had amassed $100 billion or more, anointing him as the world's first "Centibillionaire." Elon Musk was another savvy businessman who managed to grow his net worth into the Centibillionaire stratosphere during the pandemic.

Stocks, such as tech and cryptocurrency, grew tremendously, and I witnessed people change tax brackets from smart investments. I even began to do some day trading. I, like many others, made and lost a few dollars, but gained invaluable experience by stepping outside of the box and taking risks.

The scammers viewed the internet like having a personal ATM to access from their phones and laptops. I even got taken down for a few dollars. Someone had the nerve to jack my Instagram with Ransomware. This fool tried to make me pay to get my info back. I replied with and email that said, "I respect your hustle, but don't make me put the Feds on your stupid ass!"

Needless to say, he left me alone after that. Again, that was a loss that led to a lesson. I began to educate myself on antivirus software, firewalls, changing passwords, backing up data, and cloud services. This is the technology age, after all, and these things should not be taken lightly.

I am like my father when it comes to thieves: "Why take what we can make?" That's why I respect anyone's hustle, but I hate thieves. We Washingtons are stomp down hustlers who can earn a living on any end of the spectrum—from shoveling shit in the stalls, to owning the horse running the race. We can sell ice to Eskimos and water to whales (Oookay, my dad has mastered these skills. I'm still perfecting mine.) However, I have the genetics of a hustler, so don't sleep! I'm developing my mind frame to earn my own slice of the American Pie! And as my dad would say, "It's only a dream if you don't have a detailed plan of implementation, followed up by strategic execution."

***

I DECIDED THERE WAS no way that I was going to sit around doing nothing while we waited for the pandemic to end. I saw others benefitting and thriving from the changing landscape of business. I knew I had to design a way to scale my business as well. I didn't intend to be selfish or ignore the needs of others, but I understood that as an entrepreneur, I had better get with the innovative process of business and cutting-edge intelligence or get left behind. As my father would say: "There are three kinds of people: Those who do it. Those who talk about doing it. And those who wish they could do it."

The rest were probably just sitting around watching and hating on those actually in the field. I agree with Lil Wayne's lyric that says: "I'd rather be blind than standing around watching!"

I concluded that what we were experiencing was either the end of the world or the new normal. Either way, I knew from history that the water faucet would soon be turned off. What goes up must come down, and the economy was no different.

The money infusion was soon followed by Fed rate hikes, inflation, and supply chain issues that stifled the low-level businessman's ability to power up. (They had to get all that money back somehow.) In my dad's era, they liked to call that play the "flim flam." That meant that the blind or gullible would have been sold a dream, robbed for the buy money, and taxed for the experience, before they even realized what hit them. In the end, you'd find yourself even worse off than before the play began. Have you heard, "A fool and his money will soon be parted"?

***

PRIOR TO THE GLOBAL shutdown, 100% of ABC's anti-bullying work was done in person. While we were trying to service all demographics, our primary clients had been the underprivileged, urban, inner-city schools. In a nutshell, the poorest communities. Because our services are free to the schools, we absorb the cost through our public, private, and corporate donors. Yet we still don't receive enough funding to provide services to everyone who requests our program. However, I am proud to say that to date, our nonprofit, AntiBully Crusaders, has serviced over 90,000 students nationwide (primarily in Texas and Michigan).

In the previous (pre-pandemic) school year, (according to a Youth Risk Behavior Surveillance report by the DHHS and Centers for Disease and Prevention), 20.1 percent of students nationwide had experienced bullying on school property. During that same period, 16.2 percent of students were electronically bullied through email, chat rooms, instant messages, websites, and texts. On average 4,400 students commit suicide annually, and 2 out of 9 as the result of an act of bullying.

During these troubling times, the loss of life and livelihood, uncertainty and isolation, forced those of us in the education industry to find a new medium to deliver quality education to our youth. Keeping in mind that when things are somewhat back to normal, we'll still be faced with the same problems of bullying that we had prior to the pandemic, the ABC staff, my dad, and I began working day in and day out to devise a plan of action to bring our platform and services online. The plan was to produce an effective, cost-efficient, and sustainable method of operation that we could also use in the future.

Our first thought was to join forces with our schools, whom we assumed already, had the infrastructure in place. To our surprise, they were met with a plethora of complexities and challenges that we were able to learn from. Most inner-city schools lacked the technological capabilities to service students online. Educators were not equipped or skilled in online teaching platforms. Nor were students used to online learning. (Most students only use the internet for search engine assistance, shopping, or various forms of entertainment...not learning.) Because most curriculums were not designed to be taught online, learning from home wasn't interactive or fun.

We all know that students retain more information when learning is fun. Capitalizing on the deficiencies in our learning institutions and industry counterparts, ABC was able to innovatively convert our style of teaching into a virtual content format that met the needs of the pandemic environment.

The ubiquitous nature of the internet allowed us to include more strategic partnerships and simultaneously reach a broader audience. Through this dynamic collaboration with students, parents, facilitators, and prominent figures in the community, we were able to deepen the anti- bullying dialogue. This helped to transform the ways of thinking and the perspective of all the participants.

During this time, ABC hosted several small, private online sessions via Zoom. Those sessions became so intense that we were unable to broadcast live or post them because of the personal content and the need to protect the sensitive information and experiences being shared. This confidentiality was a part of our appeal to the student participants.

To accommodate the masses demanding our service, however, we hosted a series of online "Bully Free Safe Zone Summits." Our panels included children, young adults, anti-bullying advocates, business owners, law enforcement, civic leaders, educators, and parents. Our students also got a chance to have in-depth conversations with our celebrity guests.

Learning that icons were normal people who shared similar experiences really helped students to overcome their reservations and open up to share their own experiences. It was more successful than we anticipated. Our program, spread by word of mouth, overwhelmed our resources, current capabilities, and our ability to meet the demand.

I was excited, and so was my dad. We still faced the one major hurdle, however: financing. While our teaching methods and strategic partnerships set ABC apart from many industry experts, our primary challenge remained the same. Each year, since our inception, we've received more requests for services than we are able to provide due to the lack of funding.

In other businesses, this isn't always a bad problem to have. All you have to do is find financing to fill orders or expand the service to already paying customers. In the nonprofit sector, you have to find a way to absorb those costs, in order to provide a free service.

Thus, there is never a positive aspect to being underfunded. I hate telling the kids that we can't visit their schools this year, or that there's an extensive waiting list.

As the pandemic began to wane and restrictions loosened, schools reopened for in-person learning. Kids were out of school for nearly a year. In some parts of the country, even longer. Just as we predicted, the lack of social interaction created a behavioral problem in many students. Not just with the youth, but people in general.

The general public seemed to be out of control. As the influx of unemployment and stimulus money dried up, robbery, assault, and theft crimes spiked across the country. Cruelty seemed to be at an all-time high, and everyone was on edge. Our learning institutions seemed to display this problem more than anywhere else.

The shift into uncertainty compounded the social issues that existed prior to the pandemic and weren't being properly addressed (i.e., how could students concentrate on learning when they were being picked on, assaulted, having their property taken, or experiencing personal issues at home?). Schools are not properly equipped to deal with these prevalent social issues. Teachers are not clinical psychologists. We cannot expect them to effectively resolve problems that they were not trained to diagnose. ABC had to consider these factors as we stepped in and attempted to assist with the newly upgraded anti-bullying educational platform.

***

GOD DID! AS THE Lord would have it, our persistence and resilience paid off. The pandemic had stolen nearly three years of our lives, but that time played out like the eight-minute DJ Khalid, Jay-Z, and crew BANGER! It had substance! Life dealt us lemons, and we chose not to complain. We added them to the mix and made lemon iced tea. Sweet, delicious lemon iced tea! Then we bottled and sold it.

Our method was to work overtime to expand the ABC platform to include a Children's Literature publishing arm (ABC Interactive Publishing), then write, illustrate, and publish over a dozen educational children's books, such as *Benjamin Treehouse: Kid President*, *Walk Between the Raindrops*, *Meet June... The First Male Ladybug*, and *The Weeping Willow and the Laughing Hyena*.

We also managed to find ways to offer our services to women's shelters and community projects, donate hundreds of thousands of dollars in merchandise, and of course write a book about my life experiences as a woman influenced, in my pursuit of greatness, by my incarcerated father. As my dad always says: "Adversity doesn't define us. It merely exposes who we truly are. Troubling times only strengthen us for the next leg of our journey."

Chapter Twenty-Five:
Success (The Answers Are in You)

ECENTLY IT SEEMS THAT I've been asked more times than I care to mention, "What is your definition of success?" I'm thinking, *Why ask me? I'm no authority on what constitutes success. I'm still looking for it myself.*

Nevertheless, I can tell you this: Over the years, my career choices have taken me down many roads, but my plan has always been clear. I have the desire to help people. First as a student activist (against bullying). Then as an entrepreneur. Now, as a philanthropist, continuing to act as a voice for those with unmet needs and restricted access to information and education. By default, due to having an incarcerated father and brother, I have also become an advocate for prison and sentencing reform; in the fight to change institutional, social, and systemic injustices.

Obviously, we all have different opinions of what true success looks like. Whatever those differences, I'm sure of this: Who you know, or what you own, are not the true measures of who or what YOU are!

To me, being successful is the ongoing process of striving to become more, so that you can do more. It's the opportunity to continue to grow socially, economically, mentally, intellectually, and spiritually, while contributing in some meaningful way to help others. Thus, the road to becoming truly successful is always under construction. It's a progressive course—not an end to be reached. My journey has not been without difficulties and failures, but when I analyze the woman I have become, I feel a sense of awe. My perseverance and the content of my character have not been damaged by hardships. I am humbled by this realization. Good and bad will happen to us all, and once you've solved one problem, another will arise. That's just the nature of things. (Thus the saying goes: "Life is 10% what happens to you, 90% how you react to it.") So the way in which we handle the unexpected turns is what's important.

I firmly believe that it all begins with the things we are taught and exposed to as children. These experiences shape and mold our personal beliefs and expectations. Our motivations, desires, and fears are developed from these encounters. The key is to acquire the proper values, principles, and education for successful behaviors at an early age. This is called building character. Then as we become older, the natural progression of things should make us wiser.

James Allen wrote: "I am the master of my abilities." In conjunction with this understanding, we should recognize that skills reflect the "ability" we possess to perform certain actions. Actions (good or bad) are what produce results. Success is the result of an effective set of skills. In addition to the skills we already possess, we also have the capacity to obtain and develop new talents and gifts. Each of us has untapped potential and an abundance of possibilities within.

It has been an honor and a profound journey to share my life experiences with you. Even if my journey has not been relatable or relative to your circumstances, I need you to hear this if you've heard nothing else: The most important thing I've learned from my father's wisdom is that "THE ANSWERS ARE IN YOU." And as they are in me, they are in YOU also.

***

MY FATHER OFTEN tells me that he's in a good place, physically, mentally, and spiritually. For a long time I couldn't understand how he could find peace after being in prison for nearly three decades. I needed him to explain this to me.

He said, "Happiness cannot be contingent upon where you're at physically, or you'll ignore the power of mental and spiritual joy. The principles you live by create the world you live in. If you change the principles you live by, you change your world. We all have the power to change our conditions, but it starts with the mind. Everyone desires the power to alter conditions. We may not all desire to rule nations or run corporations, but we all want to get results in our lives."

Again, I was awestruck by the correlation between what he was experiencing in prison and I was experiencing in free society. It all boiled down to perspective.

In the process of attempting to master something, most of our failures don't just come from unrealistic plans or unachievable goals. We often fail to utilize our thinking ability to alter the circumstances to our benefit. A winning hand in one card game can represent a losing hand in another. Thinking outside the box often requires an objective and realistic view of the circumstances in addition to an unconventional approach to gaining an advantage. (Remember the example of selling picks, pans, and shovels while everyone else is mining for gold?)

The key is to gather information, combine it with common sense and sound judgement, and be realistic about our personal limitations. Then strategize accordingly. I believe that the main difference between winners and losers is attitude. Winners refuse to accept losing, and losers refuse to do whatever it takes to win. In this respect, winning becomes an attitude and losing becomes a lifestyle.

I've learned that some of the most successful people are the ones who have learned from their mistakes and turned their failures into opportunities. Every failure either eliminates an ineffective method or suggests a more effective approach, right? That's a positive.

My dad once wrote to me while I was in college: "Success is a journey, not a destination. The happiest people I've ever met are those who were working towards specific objectives."

I'm now experiencing that feeling of fulfillment and joy as I write my story. Until recently I hadn't considered that I might have a story-in-the-making that was actually worth telling. This has taught me that happiness is a byproduct of who you are, what you do, and how you do it.

I've found that what makes me most happy is being in a position to help others be happy. The rich and wealthy who can't seem to find happiness typically don't find themselves doing enough to help others, or they're doing too much to help the wrong people.

I'm more focused than I've ever been. I'm more ready for life than I've ever been. The lessons I've learned in the last seven years have given me that deliberateness, that self-control, the emotional intelligence, and the courage I need to achieve SUCCESS—and not just experience minor victories. I have become the "extra-miler," and I'm certainly a better team player with confidence in what I bring to the table. (Sometimes I bring the table!)

I know that true success is not instantaneous. It comes over time. However, the process has been exhilarating as well as liberating, and the many changes in my life have already been rewarding.

Closing Thoughts

WHILE THIS BOOK IS dedicated to my father for his wisdom, assistance, love, and support, even while physically absent during most of my life, I have to thank my mother and a host of relatives and family and friends for being there for me during my journey. Thank you all for supporting, respecting, and understanding my relationship with my dad.

Most of all, I want to thank you all for your patience and for loving me with all my flaws. I can't imagine what my life would have been like without you all and I wouldn't trade a single person who has been on our team. I promise that when I become the success story that you helped design, I won't forget what got me there. (I won't change, but my address certainly will.)

In this book, I've tried to share the life lessons that came from my father (who happens to be incarcerated) with the rest of the world in hopes that you may benefit from our relationship as well. During my rite of passage into adulthood, those lessons have helped to shape me into the woman I am today. During this never-ending voyage, I've learned that everyone has the potential to be great. Sometimes it takes others to bring out the best in us. Outside elements help us to identify, develop, cultivate, and master those aptitudes that we possess or are seeking.

To my family, friends, and well-wishers: I am grateful for your support and would love to hear your comments, critiques, and suggestions. Hit me up on Instagram @its.lauriee .

I have to close this with Thanks be to God! Thanks again to my sisters, my mom, and my dad. Dad: One day I hope to make you and Mama proud!

"The best is yet to come...I am you and you are me!"

Your Loving Daughter,

Lauren "Pooh" Washington.

Lauren Washington

The Lioness (From the loins of a lion...)
By J.C. Williams

If a lion growls before he bites, he'll never make the kill,

There's no food out there in the jungle waiting, sitting still,

The words "hunger" and "appetite" mean, WORK FOR EVERY MEAL.

Lying in wait for things to eat is just part of the drill.

His furry mane and fearless stride keeps the pride in check.

However, it's his LIONESS that earns him his respect.

While he's asleep, she's wide awake; more vicious than she looks,

The agile females hunt for food; she doesn't clean or cook.

In fact, she's capable of being Queen, no different from the man.

The Lion King relies on her...oh, now you understand!

Appendix A
My List of Cherished "Dadisms"

- "We plan and God plans. He's a way better planner than we are." I have learned to roll with the punches when my best plans don't go as planned. In the end, even losses can be lessons.

- "Every milestone should be recognized, but graduating is nothing to celebrate." This one was self-fulfilling. Thirteen years ago, I thought that graduating was like winning a championship. It was the start of something. Not the end.

- "No athlete is satisfied with just winning his first game when he's focused on a championship. Anything less is just part of a journey. Only losers celebrate every small accomplishment because they ain't used to winning." Proper preparation prevents poor performance.

- "Adversity builds character." Amen to that!

- "Friends and family will drag you through the mud. You gotta love 'em but you ain't gotta do business with 'em." This is even more evident now that I look back on my accomplishments and realize that my "team" was hand-picked, not related by blood.

- "Barack Obama wasn't the president when he and Michelle first met." I see this as a declaration that any man will reach a higher potential with a woman like me on his team. He can be "amazing" already, and I will help him to be like Barack: "Incomparable."

- "The problem with most relationships is that people forget how to be friends." I'm determined to overcome this challenge.

- "Anger fueled by ambition for resolution, helps you to overcome obstacles and challenges. Every move gotta be your best move. So you gotta figure out how to move, before you move, in order to win." I'm such a planner that even my plans have plans. Every move is strategic. Trust me!

- "People have a strong propensity to follow their own desires and inclinations over your personal objectives and goals, so when dealing with them you gotta leave room for error and compensate by having a contingency plan in place." Contingencies are best utilized BEFORE tragedies. Go hard first, then partner up with capable people.

- "You're too busy trying to look rich, instead of getting rich! You need to be on a ramen noodle budget and stack your chips." I'm still working on this one. I'll probably never try the ramen noodle diet, but it ain't all Kobe steak these days.

- "You don't need material things to validate your worth. Those things will come with time. You'll acquire and accumulate them while hustling." Look at me, Dad! Isn't there a middle ground?

- "Never expose to anyone how you make your money, and especially don't introduce them to your plug or clientele." I truly get it! People will steal your ideas.

- "It's not what you know, it's who you know. Your network is your net worth!" Teamwork makes the dream work!

- "After you've been separated for long periods of time, people have to be reevaluated because people change." That doesn't mean years, either! Small losses or successes alter people's personalities. Friends become foes easily when growth is involved.

- "What common people see is the end result of a production. They never consider all the details of the hard work, or blood, sweat, and tears that go into making something a success." I realize that most of my sacrifices and accomplishments will go unnoticed. I allow the self-gratification to be reward enough.

- "If you wanna be great, you gotta do all the extraordinary things that great people do. When everyone else is playing, you gotta be putting in work. When everyone else is on vacation, you gotta be putting in work. When everyone else is sleeping, you gotta be up putting in work."

- Self-employed, college degree, multiple business owner, humanitarian, author, and independent Black Woman. It's not enough to just wanna be great, you gotta put in the work! "Anything for free costs way too much!"

- "Lean on your strengths and learn to manage your weaknesses." Rinse and repeat.

- "You can have all the knowledge in the world, but it's useless if you can't put it into practicality. Apply it so that it benefits you." This applies to life in general.

- "You're not anywhere near the realm of wealth unless you have at least five streams of revenue." I'm thinking ten.

- "Never make exceptions to the rules. When you do, you leave room for errors." Rule #1: Shut up and listen! Information is potential power.

- "Have you ever noticed that the people who have been through the most shit always have the most answers?" A hell of a trade off, but it's true!

- "It's not your job to reinvent the wheel. It's your job to improve the wheel. If you don't have a new invention, service, or product, you hustle off the hustle, or become a disruptor." Changed my perspective forever.

- "If you find something you love to do and improve the process so it's more proficient or cutting edge, the money will follow." True.

- "I'd rather have enough money in the bank to purchase everything I want than to simply have everything I want." Hmmm?

- "Jealousy is the worst of all hates because you never know exactly why a person hates you. It could be your car, your hair, your man, or something as trivial as your beautiful smile. It could be anything." Watch out for the haters…they bear watching!

- I'd like to end with: "I am you and you are me..." I love you, Dad!

Appendix B
Financial Literacy

Here are a few financial tips gleaned from my personal experiences that I wish someone had taught me sooner:

- BUDGETING is a lifelong skill. Teaching young adults how to budget their money can help them plan responsible spending, save money, achieve goals, and address financial anxiety.

- ELEMENTARY SCHOOL TIPS: If you have younger kids, they likely don't have a steady income, but you can still help them understand the concept of budgeting by using their allowance as the template. Keep it simple. Teach them to track the money they receive and separate it into "spend now" and "spend later" categories. (Lunch money for the school week can be an example of "spend later" money.)

- Focus on basics, like saving. (Promising to match whatever money is left over from the previous allowance is a great incentive for kids to save.) As children begin to learn the fundamentals of math, you can introduce them to the concept of formulating a spending plan. Apply these lessons to toys or gifts they want, and teach them to set aside small amounts until they have enough to make the purchase.

- MIDDLE SCHOOL TIPS: Later, as they become young adults, you'll need to expand those categories. Teach them to measure these categories against their total monthly income (from part-time jobs, allowances, gifts, etc.). Ideally, they should have more money coming in than going out. This process will help identify "must-have" versus "want-to-have" purchases. Ultimately, this will highlight areas where they can cut back on spending in order to save. These early mathematical lessons based around spending can be expanded to real-life decision-making and budget creation. This includes what should be accounted for, and considered, prior to making purchases. Before your children go to the mall with friends, discuss the thought process involved in their spending, before they are tempted to make impulse purchases.

- *SAVE REGULARLY AND CONSISTENTLY. It's never too early to open a savings account. Making consistent, automatic contributions to a savings account can create a mindset that is invaluable to your children, as they get older. Even if your child doesn't have bills or other financial obligations, teach them to set aside some of the money from their allowance and even gifts from family or friends.

- Helping children learn to save early on, even for small purchases, can teach them to develop consistent saving habits over time.

- HIGH SCHOOL TIPS: As adulthood begins to draw nearer, it's worth exploring the fundamentals of credit scores, credit cards, investing, saving for retirement, homeownership, and more, so that upon graduation, teens can start putting those lessons into practice. High school seniors should also educate themselves on student loans, as debt soon becomes a reality for those who attend college.

- Understanding the facts can help them make more informed choices. If your high school child has a job, even if only part-time, it will be helpful to discuss taxes and how to manage a consistent income. This can guide them in creating and balancing accurate budgets in the future.

- COLLEGE STUDENT TIPS: Build credit by opening a credit card account to help achieve goals that require credit later in life, such as purchasing a home. With a career just a few years away (or sooner), college is also a perfect time to start reading into the basics of 401(k)s, starting an emergency fund, or even learning the fundamentals of investing.

- *EMPHASIZE THE IMPORTANCE of safe credit. Young adulthood is the right time to begin building credit because establishing good credit takes time. Building credit from a young age will help pave the way for major purchases and life moments. Personal credit scores impact future housing rental or purchase arrangements, the ability to obtain a new car and even employment opportunities. Teach your children the steps they can take to start building credit, such as strategizing their credit card usage and never spending outside their means.

- It's also very important to pay credit card bills on time and in-full. Young adults should also take advantage of credit card rewards programs by understanding how they work and the optimal times to capitalize on those that apply.

- Every stage of school is designed to help children prepare for lifelong success. Learning about finances is the one area that can be especially impactful in the long term. Taking the time now to teach your children strong financial habits will help them to develop lifelong financial skills. The healthy habits they build today will carry them tomorrow and beyond, ensuring your children the ability to thrive as fiscally responsible adults.